PICNIC!

◆

Recipes and Menus for Outdoor Enjoyment

▼▼▼▼▼▼▼▼▼▼▼▼▼▼▼▼▼▼▼▼▼

BY EDITH STOVEL

Cover photo by Nicholas Whitman
Cover design by Leslie Morris Noyes
Designed and produced by Leslie Morris Noyes
Illustrations by Brent Cardillo
Edited by Constance Oxley

The name Garden Way Publishing is licensed to Storey Communications, Inc., by Garden Way, Inc.

Printed in the United States Capital City Press
First printing, February, 1990

Library of Congress Catalog Card Number: 89-46014
International Standard Book Number: 0-88266-587-1 (hc); 0-88266-586-3 (pbk)

Library of Congress Cataloging-in-Publication Data

Stovel, Edith, 1940-
        PICNIC! : recipes and menus for outdoor enjoyment / by
        Edith Stovel.
            p. cm.
        ISBN 0-88266-587-1
        ISBN 0-88266-586-3 (pbk)
        1. Outdoor cookery. 2. Picnicking. I. Title.
TX823.S83 1990   89-46014
641'.3–dc20   CIP

PICNIC!

◆

Recipes and Menus for Outdoor Enjoyment

▼▼▼▼▼▼▼▼▼▼▼▼▼▼▼▼▼▼▼▼

BY EDITH STOVEL

A GARDEN WAY PUBLISHING BOOK

STOREY

STOREY COMMUNICATIONS, INC.

SCHOOLHOUSE ROAD

POWNAL, VERMONT 05261

RECIPE CREDITS FOR <u>PICNIC!</u>

Recipe on page 58 from **The Search for the Perfect Chocolate Chip Cookie** by Gwen Steege, Storey Publishing, 1988.

Recipe on page 73 from **Garden Way's Joy of Gardening Cookbook** by Janet Ballantyne, Garden Way Inc., 1984.

Recipe on page 78 based on a recipe from **The Moosewood Cookbook** by Mollie Katzen, Ten Speed Press, 1977.

Recipe on page 88 reprinted by permission of the Junior League of Palo Alto, California, from **A Private Collection.**

Recipe on page 32 reprinted by permission from **The Frog Commissary Cookbook** by Steve Poses and Rebecca Roller, The Commissary, Inc., 1985. Used by permission of Doubleday, a division of Bantam, Doubleday, Dell Publishing Group, Inc.

Recipes on page 99, page 100, and page 101 printed by permission of the Oakville Grocery Co., Oakville, California.

Recipes on pages 102 and 103 are printed by permission of the ABC Bakery in Napa, California.

All recipes in the Fall Foliage in New England Picnic reprinted by permission of Irene Maston, chef/owner, of Truffles & Such Inc., Pittsfield, Massachusetts.

Recipes on pages 111 - 115 are printed by permission of *Crosby's* of Lenox, Massachusetts.

CONTENTS

7
ACKNOWLEDGMENTS

9
WHAT IS A PICNIC?

Picnics in Art and History
Picnic Memories

11
PICNIC LOGISTICS

Packing to Go
Checklist
The Perfect Picnic Basket
Rainy Day Alternatives

15
A NOTE ABOUT THE RECIPES

17
TYPES OF PICNICS

18
PICNICS IN A PACK

Autumn Day-Hike Picnic
Winter Cross-Country Ski Picnic
Spring Day-Hike Picnic
Summer Canoe Picnic
Berry-Picking Picnic

47
WORK
PICNICS

Spring Lunch Picnic
Winter Lunch Picnic

59
POTLUCK PICNICS

Family Celebration Picnic in the
Backyard
Neighborhood Poolside Picnic
Après Ski Picnic
Friends on a Mountainside Picnic
Reunion on an Island Picnic
Sports Booster Picnic

97
STORE-BOUGHT PICNICS

California Wine Country Picnic
— *Oakville Grocery*
Fall Foliage in New England Picnic
— *Truffles & Such*
Summer in the Berkshires Picnic
— *Crosby's*

116
SANDY PICNICS

Spring Breakfast on the Beach
Picnic
Summer Beach Picnic
Autumn Beach Picnic

133
ELEGANT PICNICS

Musical Festival Picnic
After the Wedding Brunch Picnic
Champagne Tea Picnic
Garden Picnic

156
ROMANTIC PICNICS

Breakfast in a Meadow Picnic
Sunlight Through the Trees Picnic
Moonlight on a Mountaintop Picnic

173
INDEX

ACKNOWLEDGMENTS

Gathering people around good food in a lovely setting was what family meant to my mother, Beatrice McCoy. She was locally known as a good cook. Seemingly without effort, she produced wonderful meals for family and friends. Her admonition to never economize on food remains with me, even though I know it is possible to do so and still enjoy great food. We must all eat to live, but in my family the emphasis was on living to eat. My mother was an artist who loved to cook. Her artistry was expressed in the care with which she prepared food and the beauty of its presentation. I am grateful to her.

My husband, Jack, willingly was the chief sampler of picnic fare. My daughters, Kate and Meg, participated in many picnics, and also helped test and review recipes. Their help and encouragement was invaluable. And I must also say that I appreciate my friends and family who sampled recipes, commented on the food and menus, gave ideas for recipes, and joined us in memorable picnics.

Bob West, owner of West Liquor Store in North Adams, Massachusetts, a small spirit shop known for its fine, moderately priced wines, has a talent for choosing the perfect wine to complement a meal. He kindly read the menus and recommended the wines included in the book.

My appreciation also goes to Eric Murray of the *Oakville Grocery* in Oakville, California, to Bobbi Crosby of *Crosby's* in Lenox, Massachusetts, and Irene Maston of *Truffles & Such,* Pittsfield, Massachusetts, for generouly sharing recipes for this book.

These recipes are a reflection of growing up on the East Coast and living in New England for many years. There is also a strong California connection based on one year of residence, many visits, and a growing fascination with the climate, land, and abundance of intriguing foods and recipes — thus, the bicoastal flavor to this book.

WHAT IS A PICNIC?

▼▼

PICNICS IN ART AND HISTORY

The history of picnics or eating outdoors is visually evident when one strolls through a museum of European paintings. Recall the images of great outdoor eating and drinking extravaganzas among the peasants in Bruegel's works. The impressionists, particularly Monet and Manet, were fond of depicting romantic meals in secluded gardens. The most striking and well-known impressionist picnic painting is Manet's *Le Dejeuner Sur L'Herbe,* Picnic on the Grass, where the food was clearly not the main focus of that afternoon. Dining outdoors evokes festivity or romance even though in some cases, it is dictated by the necessity of cooking out of doors.

Historically, picnics were meals where each person contributed something to the total repast. This idea of a "potluck" meal goes back to the Greek word *syncomist* which means "brought from different places and put together." A syncomist initially was a coarse bread made of the by-products of flour. Syncomist was expanded to designate a meal in common to which everyone brings something, or a picnic.

These communal meals spread throughout the continent and were enjoyed by Scandinavians, Germans, and French. The picnic as an English institution was first described in the early nineteenth century as a fashionable social entertainment to which everyone brought something. The institution evolved to include excursion parties to the country where all contributed food, or one person may have provided the entire picnic. In the early nineteenth century, the English also had a Picnic Society devoted to entertainment and theatricals as well as dining, where each member contributed something. The English, French, as well as other Europeans, continue this tradition of outdoor dining.

Our present day concept of a sandwich is often associated with portable meals or picnics. The idea of a sandwich as a snack goes back to Roman times. Scandinavians perfected the technique with the Danish open-faced sandwich or *smorrebrod,* consisting of thinly sliced, buttered bread and many delectable toppings. These elaborate concoctions are not as portable as their sturdy American counterparts, but can be constructed on site and are highly suitable for an elegant picnic. The Earl of Sandwich, John Montagu, the eighteenth century gambler, who was known to have sat at the gaming table for twenty-four hours with nothing more than roast beef placed between two slices of toast for his nourishment, is the person to whom we are indebted for putting a top on the sandwich.

PICNIC MEMORIES

When I asked people to describe their favorite picnic, heads tilted back, eyes shut, and smiles crept across faces. One person described the adventure of family picnics. When her parents first announced a family picnic, they all jumped into the car loaded with a picnic basket. Her father began driving, turning right, then left, then right and so on as the excitement mounted, and finally they came to the "picnic spot." Whether her father had a predetermined spot in mind is irrelevant. The memory of these childhood excursions remains vivid.

After a long hard week of work, one friend recalled a starlight picnic on a hill within walking distance of home. The toils of the week melted under the soothing starlight. Another evening picnic with a romantic twist was in the moonlight on the beach at Half Moon Bay in California.

My brother reminisced about backyard birthday picnics with the special tall birthday cake mounded high with boiled icing that became crunchy on the outside the next day, if there was ever any left over. I remember family picnics on a small bay in Rhode Island where our friends ordered a huge clam bake. An enormous drum, which we heated on an open fire by the water, contained lobsters on top, followed by many layers of steamed vegetables and fish. The prize at the bottom was tender steamed clams in the delicious broth made by all the preceding layers.

An old-fashioned picnic is recalled by the annual croquet match between the U.S. Naval Academy and St. John's College in Annapolis, Maryland. This polite athletic contest is followed by an elegant picnic on the lawn.

My most unusual picnic was eaten on a bus crossing the desert. After a delightful week in Ogden, Utah, our hostess packed us a picnic lunch of antelope sandwiches on which we gratefully munched as we crossed the Great Salt Lake and Nevada desert on the way to San Francisco.

A picnic evokes leisure time, relaxation, and enjoyment of the outdoors. It can be a still life in the open air or a boisterous frolic on the beach. Some picnics celebrate a special occasion, some offer the opportunity for friends to gather, and others provide an excuse for breaking the routine of daily life. In all cases, the food is transportable and the excitement is palpable. Ask someone to go on a picnic with you and watch their eyes light up. A picnic is more than eating a meal, it is a pleasurable state of mind. Let's go on a picnic means "let's have fun."

The people, the place, and the food are the essential ingredients of a memorable picnic. A truly magnificent picnic consists of dear friends or family, a spectacular setting, and delectable food and drink. You choose the companions and the site, and this book will provide you with recipes and ideas for the food and the presentation. Picnic entertaining allows you to truly enjoy the occasion because everything is done ahead. All you must do then is enjoy the setting, your companions, and, of course, the food.

PICNIC LOGISTICS

▼▼

PACKING TO GO

THE FOOD
▼▼▼▼▼▼▼▼▼▼▼▼

What differentiates a picnic from other meals is that it is packed to go. The packing of the food and accoutrements becomes a key part of the planning. The cooking and preparation is completed in advance. The food is stored in containers that will keep it safe, appetizing, and ready to serve at the desired temperature. The cook does not have to deal with the last-minute-panic of wondering if all the dishes will be ready at the same time and at the right temperature.

At the end of each recipe, you will find special packing tips. Safety is the main issue. Preventing bacterial growth which could cause illness can be accomplished by observing some simple procedures. Since picnic food often goes for long periods of time without direct heat or conventional refrigeration, observing sanitary practices in preparation and storage activities becomes particularly important. Clean hands and work surfaces are basic. Keeping fresh foods in the refrigerator before and after preparation is essential. Using vinegars, lemon juice, and acidic ingredients in recipes is a useful way to avoid bacterial growth. Keeping hot foods hot and cold foods cold is the goal for both safety and appeal.

Preparing foods that will be served cold is the least complicated. Foods can be prepared, placed in traveling containers, and refrigerated or frozen until time to pack the picnic basket. The problem of soggy sandwiches can be eliminated by wrapping the bread in a plastic bag and packing the filling ingredients separately, then chilling them in the cooler. All cold food should be refrigerated until it is **thoroughly** cold. With meat, poultry, or fish that is to be grilled, it could be carried frozen to the picnic in the cooler and slowly thawed en route. Do not let meats, poultry, or fish thaw at room or air temperature because bacteria can form on the warm outer surfaces. Cold food can be packed in cold thermos bottles, coolers with ice or freezer packs, or wrapped in heavy tablecloths, quilts, or layers of newspaper and placed in the picnic basket with a chunk of ice.

On our family camping trips we created chunks of ice by thoroughly cleaning half-gallon cardboard milk containers, almost filling them with water, and freezing them the night before we left. The chunk of ice lasted about a day, and the melt-water provided a refreshing drink for tired, thirsty campers. You can see the necessity of cleaning the container first. Plan to bring your own water supply as even the most sparkling streams may be polluted with animal bacteria or chemical waste. In hot weather, if people will be exercising, sufficient amounts of water are essential.

Packing food that should be served hot is more of a challenge. For liquids, bring the food to as high a temperature as you can and then pour it into a thermos bottle which you have just rinsed with boiling water. For other foods, also bring them to a high temperature and then wrap them in heavy-duty aluminum foil and place them in an insulated bag or a heavy cloth. If you can keep the food at 140°F., it should be quite safe. For winter picnics at subfreezing temperatures, this can be difficult. With hot foods, it is best not to bring home leftovers. For cold foods, leftovers can be packed in the cooler for not more than four hours. Remember the old adage, when in doubt, throw it out. Eat all you bring, but bring plenty of food because fresh air enhances the appetite. Plan well and cook well and there won't be many leftovers.

THE OTHER ITEMS
▼▼▼▼▼▼▼▼▼▼▼▼▼

Besides carefully chosen and prepared food, a picnic includes the plates, the flatware, colorful napkins, tablecloths, and cups. Essentials include matches and garbage bags. Special touches are fresh flowers, mints, and candles. Create a perfect summer day by combining good company and good food in a beautiful setting. Don't forget the corkscrew. To avoid forgetting an essential item, a checklist is helpful, and a prepacked picnic basket is even better because then you can be spontaneous and just grab your basket and go. With all these notes on preparation, remember that a picnic is fun. Don't get overburdened with the planning so that you don't want to bother with the picnic. Do it in a way that suits your style and inclination.

A note for the environment: Care for the land on which you have your picnic and abide by the back country rule that you leave nothing but your footprints. Avoid excess use of disposable plastics and Styrofoam. Bring a garbage bag and collect all your trash and bring it home, or leave it in an appropriate roadside trash container. See how little trash you can generate on your picnic. There are many beautiful, colorful throwaway picnic items on the market, including plates, cups, and napkins. There are also some attractive lasting ones. If you plan to picnic frequently, it will benefit both you and the environment to invest in some permanent picnicware.

CHECKLIST
▼▼▼▼▼▼▼▼▼▼▼▼▼▼

Some people choose to have their basket ready to travel so they can move at the hint of a picnic. Those people also have on hand a selection of ground covers, including reed mats, space blankets, beach towels, blankets, and quilts.

ESSENTIALS FOR THE WELL-PACKED PICNIC BASKET

plates
tableware
glassware
ground cloth, blankets, old quilts, or whatever suits your mood
paper napkins
tablecloth
garbage bag
corkscrew (for those who like wine)
paper towels
insect repellent

These items depend on your mood and style:
candles, candle holders, and matches
flowers and vase
wine glasses
china, crystal, and silverware
cloth napkins

For a slightly different approach you may refer to Mrs. Beeton's *Book of Household Management* in which she lists, "Things not to be forgotten at a picnic." Our idea of essentials is somewhat different from Mrs. Beeton's in 1859.

A stick of horseradish, a bottle of mint-sauce well corked, a bottle of salad dressing, a bottle of vinegar, made mustard, pepper, salt, good oil, and pounded sugar. If it can be managed, take a little ice. It is scarcely necessary to say that plates, tumblers, wine-glasses, knives, forks, and spoons, must not be forgotten; as also teacups and saucers, 3 or 4 teapots, some lump sugar, and milk, if this last-named article cannot be obtained in the neighbourhood. Take 3 corkscrews.

THE PERFECT PICNIC BASKET

The perfect picnic basket contains all the things you will need to create an idyllic afternoon (evening or morning) with your friends in a beautiful spot. Perfection can be achieved in many ways and planning ahead can help, but don't plan so much that you lose the sense of spontaneity which is essential to a picnic. Since you have to carry the basket, you don't want to bring everything you could possibly ever need. You want to have the things that will make this event memorable and fun. There are different baskets for different types of picnics. Since everyone will have a different image of perfection, let me share one with you.

A favorite picnic image is an antique market basket with a loose bouquet of fresh flowers poking out one corner, a bottle of wine protruding from another, a fresh tablecloth covering fresh loaves of bread, garden vegetables converted to savoury servings, chilled meats and cheeses, a luscious dessert, and steaming coffee. I like a cloth tablecloth and napkins, and depending on the occasion, enjoy colorful paper and plastic products for plates and tableware. For elegant picnics, I'd choose glassware, china, and silverware unless a hike is involved.

I personally like baskets of all sorts and shapes and am a sucker for them at antique or secondhand stores. However, there are numerous insulated bags, coolers, and cloth totes that can serve as the "perfect picnic basket." Whatever you choose, pack your basket with as much food, drink, and excitement as it will hold.

RAINY DAY ALTERNATIVES

We envisage glorious, sunny weather for our picnics, and unless we live in California or the Southwest, we cannot count on that. When the weather doesn't cooperate with our plans, there are several alternatives; we can cancel our picnic, we can reschedule it, or we can choose an alternative location under cover. In choosing the third alternative, some of our picnics may end up on the dining room table. That may result in a lovely picnic, but with some advance work, an alternative sight can be selected.

One of my favorite picnics is to gather family and friends several hours before sunset and hike a short distance up the Appalachian Trail to a beautiful meadow with a panoramic view of the mountains. In this mellow setting we can watch the kaleidoscopic sky as the sun drops into the hills. On one such occasion, the weather was threatening. It was essential to find a place with a view. We located an unused building with a wide porch on the local college campus and were prepared for our picnic adventure in the event of a storm. In this case, the weather cleared just as we left and we were able to see the sunset after all.

A porch provides a good alternative site for a rainy day picnic because there is some sense of being outdoors. On cold days, a picnic by the fire in the living room offers coziness with the relaxed atmosphere of a picnic. Sunshine and picnics go together, but watching a rainstorm from a dry porch can offer a different way to enjoy the outdoors. In planning a picnic, be aware of the weather forecasts, but think of ways to enjoy your picnic in all kinds of weather.

A NOTE ABOUT THE RECIPES

Most of the recipes are for eight people. This number is easily divided and multiplied for smaller or larger picnic parties. Some of the picnics include wine and beer suggestions, others do not. Those picnics involving physical exertion include equally attractive nonalcoholic beverage suggestions.

These are my favorite recipes which contain my favorite foods. Some go back to my grandmother's youth, many have been collected along the way from friends and family, and others are the result of my own experimentation. If you enjoy fresh foods, a well-balanced diet, have a sweet tooth, and make an effort to cut down on the sugar, salt, and fat in your diet, you may find you share my taste. These recipes do not avoid the villains of the American diet, but the amounts are kept low in most recipes.

TYPES OF PICNICS

▼▼▼▼▼▼▼▼▼▼▼▼▼▼▼▼▼▼▼▼▼▼▼

PICNICS IN A PACK

▼▼▼

One thing I love about backpacking is filling the little containers and bottles with food and drink. Packing just enough to come out even, so as not to lug excess food or trash home, is always a challenge for the backpacker. The same planning is required for a picnic in a pack. With fresh air and exercise, the picnickers will be hungry. One deserves to eat heartily after vigorous exercise. Be generous but not excessive with the food. Use lightweight food containers and bring several packs; one for cold items, one for hot, one for the food that doesn't need either cold or hot, and one for the nonfood items. Be sure that everyone gets to carry a pack.

The other thing I love about backpacking is gorp. This otherwise decadent combination of chocolate, nuts, and raisins is just what the hungry hiker needs to supply energy for the final spurt. Mix equal amounts of chocolate chips, peanuts, and raisins in a large bowl and make up a packet of gorp for each hiker. We have bribed ourselves and our children up many a mountain with the promise of gorp at rest stops.

AUTUMN DAY-HIKE PICNIC

As a New Englander, I am well aware of the appeal of this time of year when the air is golden, country roads are brilliant, and mountainsides are muted. New Englanders are driven to spend as many hours in the crisp, clear air as possible before the winter winds sweep down. Even raking leaves offers enjoyment because it is an excuse to be outdoors. But more fun is crunching through fallen leaves on a winding trail in search of a sunny spot by a stream. It is a bittersweet time of year, so beautiful and so fleeting that one should enjoy every golden moment of it. Pack a picnic and take a hike.

MENU

This menu is for a warm fall day. If the weather is cool,
then heat the soup and pour it into hot thermos bottles.

ICED BORSCHT*

THINLY SLICED DANISH HAM WITH BOURSIN*

AND GARDEN LETTUCE

ON ZESTY RYE BREAD*

ALMOND TART* WITH RUBY RED GRAPES

CIDER

EXTRA ITEMS TO BRING:

BACKPACKS

SMALL INSULATED BAG WITH ICE PACK

SPACE BLANKET

ICED BORSCHT
▼▼▼▼▼▼▼▼▼▼▼▼▼

Serves 8   Preparation Time: 45 minutes   Chilling time: 2 hours

1 quart water
8 small to medium beets, cut into equal quarters
1 tablespoon corn oil
1 tablespoon butter
1 medium onion, chopped
1 garlic clove, minced
1 tablespoon chopped fresh dill
½ teaspoon salt
¼ teaspoon white pepper
1 tablespoon lemon juice
3 cups chicken stock
2 cups buttermilk
¼ cup sour cream mixed with ¼ cup plain yogurt for topping
dill sprigs for garnish

1. Bring the water to a boil in a large saucepan. Add the beets and cook them for about 30 minutes or until tender when pierced with a fork. Drain and rinse the beets in cold water. When cool enough to touch, slip the skins off.

2. Heat the oil and butter in a large skillet over medium heat. Sauté the onion for 5 minutes or until translucent. Add the garlic and cook for 1 minute and remove from the heat. Add the dill, salt, pepper, lemon juice, and chicken stock.

3. Place some stock and some beets in a blender or food processor and puree. Pour the soup into a large bowl and repeat the processing until all of the broth and beets are pureed. Add the buttermilk, stir to blend, and chill for several hours.

4. Pour the soup into cold thermos bottles and place an ice cube in each one.

Pack the sour cream mixture in a small covered container and place it in the cooler for traveling. The dill sprigs can be transported in a seal-lock plastic bag. At serving time, pour the soup into attractive cups, top each serving with a tablespoon of the sour cream mixture, and garnish with a dill sprig.

BOURSIN
▼▼▼▼▼▼▼▼▼▼▼▼▼

Not designed for those watching their cholesterol. However, since this is so good, the trick is to eat a small amount of it. A thin layer on a slice of bread provides a wonderful background for the ham.

Makes 1½ cups   *Preparation Time: 15 minutes*   *Storage Time: 3 days*

8 ounces softened cream cheese
½ cup softened butter
1 tablespoon lemon juice
½ teaspoon Worcestershire sauce
½ teaspoon dry mustard
1 tablespoon minced fresh parsley
1 tablespoon minced fresh chives
1 teaspoon dried tarragon
1 garlic clove, minced

1. Place all the ingredients in a food processor and process until well mixed. Refrigerate the cheese for 3 days to blend the flavors.

2. Place in a 1-pint covered container and refrigerate until ready to pack the picnic.

ZESTY RYE BREAD
▼▼▼▼▼▼▼▼▼▼▼▼▼▼

A very tasty loaf that is quite dense and can be thinly sliced with ease.

Makes 2 loaves   *Preparation Time: 30 minutes*   *Rising Time: 2 hours*   *Baking Time: 30 minutes*

2 tablespoons active dry yeast
1½ cups warm water
¼ cup molasses
1 tablespoon sugar
2 tablespoons grated orange rind
¼ cup fresh orange juice
4 teaspoons fennel seeds
4 teaspoons anise seeds
½ teaspoon crushed cardamom seeds
2 tablespoons softened margarine
1 teaspoon salt
2½ cups rye flour
1½ to 2 cups all-purpose flour

1. Sprinkle the yeast over the warm water in a large bowl and let sit about 5 minutes, or until the yeast is dissolved. Mix the molasses, sugar, orange rind, orange juice, the fennel, anise, and cardamom seeds, and margarine together in a small bowl.

2. When the yeast is dissolved, add the molasses mixture to the yeast and stir to blend.

3. Add the salt and the rye flour and beat with a whisk until the flour is well blended. Gradually add the all-purpose flour, one cup at a time and beat it with a wooden spoon. When the dough seems to come to-gether in a ball in the center of the bowl and is soft, but not sticky, scrape the sides of the bowl and dump all the contents on a lightly floured surface. At this point, you will not have added the total amount of the all-purpose flour.

4. Knead the dough for about 10 minutes. As it gets sticky, add small amounts of the remaining all-purpose flour. When the dough is well kneaded, it will have absorbed most of the flour and will be smooth and round and softly firm to the touch. It should not be sticky (too little flour), or rigid (too much flour).

5. Put the dough into a clean, oiled bowl, turn the dough over to coat it with oil, cover it with a damp towel, and let it rise in a warm, draft-free place until it is double in bulk, 45 minutes to 1 hour.

6. When the dough has risen according to your schedule, punch it down and knead it two times to form a smooth shape and to release the air bubbles. Divide the dough into two equal pieces and shape each half into a smooth oval. Place the loaves on a greased baking sheet and let them rise for 1 hour.

7. Preheat the oven to 350° F.

8. Before baking, make three diagonal slashes across the top of each loaf. Bake for 30 minutes. Remove from the baking sheet and cool on a wire rack. When the bread is cool, store it in plastic bags. Slice the loaves before packing the picnic.

BODIL'S ALMOND TART
▼▼▼▼▼▼▼▼▼▼▼▼▼▼

Bodil, who is Danish and a wonderful cook, shared this recipe with me. It has been to many picnics. This delightful tart can be made quickly and packs beautifully. While you're at it, you can make two and freeze one for another picnic.

Makes one 10-inch tart   *Preparation Time: 15 minutes*   *Baking Time: 20 minutes*

CRUST:
1 cup all-purpose flour
6 tablespoons margarine
3 tablespoons confectioners' sugar

FILLING:
¼ cup margarine
½ cup sugar
2 eggs
1 to 2 teaspoons pure almond extract
1 cup chopped almonds

1. Preheat the oven to 350° F.

2. To make the crust, place the flour, margarine, and sugar in a food processor. Process the mixture until it has a crumbly appearance. Pour the crumbly mixture into a 10-inch tart pan and press it against the bottom and sides to create a uniform crust.

3. To make the filling, cream the margarine and sugar until fluffy in the large bowl of an electric mixer. Add the eggs and almond extract and continue beating until well combined. At low speed, add the almonds and mix only until blended.

4. Pour the filling into the crust and bake for 20 minutes or until the filling is set and slightly darkened. Cool in the pan on a wire rack. When the tart is cool, slice it into eight pieces and carefully wrap two pieces at a time in aluminum foil. If you make the tart well in advance, these packages could be frozen until it is time to pack the picnic.

WINTER CROSS-COUNTRY SKI PICNIC

On cold, sunny winter days the sky against the white snow seems bluer that at any other time of year. Woods filled with soft snow, intricate lace patterns of trees cut against the deep blue sky, frosty breath and rosy cheeks, and we're enjoying a day of cross-country skiing. The experience is intense and the appetites grow large. Hot, hearty food is the perfect antidote to the cold crisp air that quickly wraps around the steaming bodies as they stop for a quick lunch.

MENU
TEN BEAN SOUP*
THINLY SLICED ROAST BEEF AND SAGA BLUE CHEESE
CARETAKER FARM BREAD*
KATE AND MEG'S CHOCOLATE CHIP OATMEAL COOKIES*
THIRST QUENCHING ORANGES
HOT SPICED TEA*

EXTRA ITEMS TO BRING:
DAY PACKS
SPACE BLANKET FOR THE LUNCH STOP
THERMOS BOTTLES FOR THE SOUP
INSULATED BAGS TO KEEP THE BEEF, CHEESE, AND ORANGES FROM FREEZING
COLD WATER TO SUPPLEMENT THE ORANGES

TEN BEAN SOUP
▼▼▼▼▼▼▼▼▼▼▼▼▼

Serves 8   Preparation Time: 30 minutes   Soaking Time: Overnight   Cooking Time: 3 hours

¼ cup each dried red kidney beans, green split peas, yellow split peas, lentils, black-eyed peas, navy beans, lima beans, black turtle beans, and pinto beans (It is possible to buy these beans already mixed in a bag.)
2 tablespoons barley
water to cover
2 quarts water
1 to 2 pounds kielbasa sausage, cut into 1-inch chunks
1 bay leaf
2 garlic cloves, minced
1 medium onion, chopped
1 28-ounce can tomato puree
1 tablespoon chili powder
2 tablespoons lemon juice
½ teaspoon dried thyme
1 teaspoon dried savory
½ teaspoon salt
freshly ground black pepper

1. Wash the beans and barley thoroughly. Place them in a soup pot, cover them with the water, and soak them overnight. In the morning, drain off the water and put the beans and barley back in the pot. Add the water, sausage, bay leaf, and garlic. Bring to a boil over high heat and then simmer gently for 2½ to 3 hours, stirring occasionally

2. Add the remaining ingredients and simmer for an additional 30 minutes. Remove the bay leaf and pour into wide-mouth thermos bottles.

CARETAKER FARM BREAD
▼▼▼▼▼▼▼▼▼▼▼▼▼

Elizabeth sells this bread at her farmstand and reports that it is the favorite of her diverse customers who travel long distances to buy delicious bread, warm from her farmhouse bakery and wonderful organic vegetables, fresh from her garden.

Makes 2 loaves   Preparation Time: 1 hour   Rising Time: 2 to 3 hours   Baking Time: 30 to 40 minutes

1 cup old-fashioned rolled oats
2 cups hot water
2 tablespoons active dry yeast
½ cup warm water
¼ cup honey
3½ cups unbleached all-purpose flour
¼ cup vegetable oil
1 teaspoon salt
2 cups whole-wheat flour
¼ cup sunflower seeds (optional)
½ cup raisins (optional)

1. Mix the oats in the hot water and let the mixture stand for 30 minutes.

2. When the oats have cooled, dissolve the yeast in the warm water in a large bowl. Add the honey and 2 cups of the all-purpose flour and beat vigorously with a wooden spoon for several minutes. When the oat mixture has cooled slightly, stir it into the flour and let the mixture sit for 30 minutes.

3. Add the remaining all-purpose flour and beat well. Add the oil, salt, and half of the whole-wheat flour and beat some more. Add the remaining whole-wheat flour and the sunflower seeds and raisins and beat well. At this point, it may be difficult to beat the dough with a spoon, so it is time to put it on a floured surface for kneading.

4. Knead the dough for 10 minutes. Put the dough into a clean, oiled bowl. Turn the dough over to coat it with oil, cover it with a damp cloth, and let the dough rise in a draft-free place until it is double in bulk, 45 minutes to 1 hour.

5. Punch down the dough and return it to the floured work surface. Divide the dough in half and shape each half into a loaf. Place each loaf in a greased 9-inch-by-5-inch bread pan and set the pans in a warm place to rise. Let the loaves rise for 1 hour, or until they mound slightly above the tops of the pans.

6. Preheat the oven to 400° F.

7. Bake the loaves for 30 to 40 minutes or until golden brown and hollow sounding when tapped with your knuckles. Remove the bread from the pans and cool on wire racks. When cool, slice the loaves and place them in plastic bags for putting in your pack.

KATE AND MEG'S CHOCOLATE CHIP OATMEAL COOKIES
▼▼▼▼▼▼▼▼▼▼▼▼

Makes 3½ dozen   Preparation Time: 45 minutes   Baking Time: 10 minutes

2¼ cups all-purpose flour
1 teaspoon baking soda
½ teaspoon salt
½ cup granulated sugar
¾ cup firmly packed light brown sugar
½ cup softened unsalted butter, cut into 1-inch chunks
½ cup softened margarine, cut into 1-inch chunks
1 teaspoon pure vanilla extract
2 eggs
1½ cups old-fashioned rolled oats
1½ cups chocolate chips

1. Preheat the oven to 350° F.

2. Mix the flour, baking soda, and salt together in a large bowl.

3. In the large bowl of an electric mixer, mix the sugars together at low speed. Add the chunks of butter and margarine and continue to beat at low speed, then increase to high speed and beat until light and fluffy. Add the vanilla and eggs at low speed, then increase to high speed.

4. At low speed, add the flour mixture ½ cup at a time, then increase to high speed until the mixture is well blended. Stir in the oats and chips with a wooden spoon.

5. Drop by rounded tablespoons onto an ungreased baking sheet and bake for 10 minutes or until golden brown. Remove the cookies from the oven and cool on wire racks for a minute or two before removing them from the baking sheet. Cool cookies completely on wire racks and pack in a seal-lock plastic bag for traveling in the picnic pack.

HOT SPICED TEA

▼▼▼▼▼▼▼▼▼▼▼▼▼

Serves 8   Preparation Time: 15 minutes

6 tablespoons tea, or 6 tea bags
2 whole cardamom pods, cracked
3 whole cloves
1 stick cinnamon
1 tablespoon honey
6 cups boiling water
1 cup scalded milk

1. Place the tea, cardamom, cloves, cinnamon, and honey in a large teapot. Pour the boiling water over the tea and let sit at least for 5 minutes. Add the milk and stir well.

2. Strain the tea into two 1-quart thermos bottles and pack in the packs.

SPRING DAY-HIKE PICNIC

Tiny, early spring violets, wild lily of the valley, and bunchberry poke their blossoms through the dense leaf cover along the trail and with luck, a trillium or lady slipper appears beneath the trees. Find yourself a glade of these miniature beauties and look through the leafless trees to find a view that would be hidden in the summer. It's often too muddy to hike in the spring and the bugs can be a bother, but it's a thrill to see things growing after a long winter. Pick a sunny day with soft, balmy breezes and enjoy the chance to dine in the open air.

MENU
CORN CHOWDER*

GRILLED CHICKEN FILLETS ON DELI ROLLS*

CARROT STICKS

FRESH GINGERBREAD* AND FRUIT

HERBAL ICED TEA*

EXTRA ITEMS TO BRING:

THERMOS BOTTLES

SMALL INSULATED BAG WITH ICE PACK

BACKPACKS

INSECT REPELLENT

SPACE BLANKET

CORN CHOWDER
▼▼▼▼▼▼▼▼▼▼▼▼▼

Serves 8   Preparation Time: 30 minutes

4 slices bacon
1 medium onion, minced
4 medium potatoes, peeled and diced
2 cups water or chicken stock
2 cups creamed style corn
1 cup corn kernels
4 cups scalded milk*
3 tablespoons butter
salt and pepper to taste
2 cups grated cheddar cheese (optional)

* For a richer chowder, substitute 1 cup heavy cream for 1 cup of the milk.
For a low-calorie soup, use skim milk.

1. Place the bacon in a large kettle or Dutch oven with a cover. Cook the bacon until evenly browned. Remove the bacon from the pan and set aside. Pour off all but 1 tablespoon of the bacon fat.

2. Add the onion to the kettle and cook about 5 minutes or until slightly browned. Add the potatoes and water or stock, bring to a boil, and simmer for 10 to 15 minutes, or until the potatoes are soft.

3. Add all the corn and milk and heat thoroughly, but do not boil. Add the butter and the salt and pepper. Pour the chowder into two wide mouth thermos bottles and place in the pack. Crumble the bacon and place it in a seal-lock plastic bag. Place the cheese in another seal-lock plastic bag. After serving the soup, garnish each cup with some bacon and ¼ cup cheese.

CHICKEN FILLETS ON DELI ROLLS
▼▼▼▼▼▼▼▼▼▼▼▼▼

This chicken is also delicious without a roll. (The marinade is from *The Frog Commissary Cookbook*, 1985.)

Serves 8   Preparation Time: 15 minutes   Marinating Time: 30 minutes

8 chicken breast halves, boned and skinned
corn oil for cooking
8 deli rolls

MARINADE:
½ cup sesame oil
1 cup tamari or soy sauce
½ cup lime juice
¼ cup mirin (sweet cooking sake) *
4 large garlic cloves, minced
2 tablespoons peeled and grated fresh gingerroot
3 tablespoons crushed red pepper flakes

* Available in natural food stores

1. Rinse and pat dry the chicken and place in a low-sided glass pan.

2. Combine the marinade ingredients in a small bowl and pour over the chicken. Let sit for 30 minutes in the refrigerator.

3. Preheat the gas grill to high.

4. Remove the chicken from the marinade and brush lightly with the corn oil. Grill the chicken for 3 minutes on a side or until cooked through, brushing often with the marinade. An alternate cooking method is to sauté the chicken in a skillet with 1 tablespoon corn oil. Cook no more than 3 minutes on each side.

5. Let the chicken cool slightly and then refrigerate. Wrap the cold chicken in aluminum foil for transporting. Slice the rolls and place them in a seal-lock plastic bag. At the picnic site, put the chicken in the rolls and enjoy a hearty sandwich of tender and moist grilled chicken. The trick is not to overcook the chicken and dry it out.

GINGERBREAD
▼▼▼▼▼▼▼▼▼▼▼▼▼▼

Makes 1 square cake　　　*Preparation Time: 10 to 15 minutes*　　　*Baking Time: 25 to 35 minutes*

1 cup molasses
½ cup buttermilk
1 egg, slightly beaten
2 cups all-purpose flour
½ cup sugar
½ teaspoon salt
1 teaspoon baking soda
1 teaspoon ground ginger
1 teaspoon ground cinnamon
1 teaspoon ground allspice
½ cup melted butter
1 cup heavy cream, whipped (optional)

1. Preheat oven to 350° F.

2. In a small bowl, combine the molasses, buttermilk, and egg and stir to blend.

3. Sift the dry ingredients into a large bowl. Add the molasses mixture and mix well. Add the butter and stir until just blended.

4. Pour the batter into a greased 9-inch-by-9-inch square aluminum foil baking pan. Bake for 25 to 35 minutes, or until a tester inserted in the center comes out clean. Cool in the pan on a wire rack. When completely cool, cut into eight generous pieces and cover securely with aluminum foil for packing in the pack.

5. Put the whipped cream in a small covered container in the refrigerator until packing time. Wrap the container in heavy aluminum foil and place it in the pack.

HERBAL ICED TEA
▼▼▼▼▼▼▼▼▼▼▼▼▼

This cold infusion is refreshing on a warm spring day or in the heat of midsummer.

Makes 2 quarts   Preparation Time: 5 minutes   Chilling Time: 1 to 2 hours

6 bags of Orange Zinger, or other herbal tea
2 quarts cold water
2 tablespoons honey (optional)
lemon slices

1. Put the tea bags into a large pitcher.

2. Pour the water over the bags and add the honey if desired. Store the pitcher in the refrigerator for at least 1 hour, during which time the tea will infuse the water.

3. Remove the tea bags and pour the cold tea into thermos bottles when ready for your hike. Put the lemon slices in a seal-lock plastic bag and serve them with the cups of tea for a refreshing drink after a long hike.

SUMMER CANOE PICNIC

A hot summer day is essential for this adventure. For a mixed age group, pick a lazy stream or river and gently paddle with the current. Wear your bathing suits and bring your sense of humor for the dunking someone in the group is sure to have. Arrange to be picked up at a point downstream so you don't have to fight the current returning home.

The first challenge of a canoeing picnic is to keep the food dry as well as cold. To do this, find a large waterproof bag with a secure closing. Canoe rental outfits will often supply these bags. If you are bringing your own canoe, you have probably used your ingenuity to devise waterproof storage. Once you have your gear stowed and are enjoying the gentle flow of the river, you are ready for your second challenge — to find the perfect picnic spot and to have everyone agree to stop **before** you have paddled past it.

MENU
ICED CUCUMBER SOUP*

LEMONY CHICKEN*

RED POTATO SALAD WITH FRESH PEAS*

TANNIES* AND GRAPES

WHITE WINE SPRITZERS* OR SPARKLING CRANBERRY JUICE*

EXTRA ITEMS TO BRING:

WATERPROOF FOOD STORAGE BAG

CORKSCREW

ICED CUCUMBER SOUP
▼▼▼▼▼▼▼▼▼▼▼▼▼

Serves 8   Preparation Time: 15 minutes   Chilling Time: 1 hour

5 cucumbers, peeled, seeded, and cut into 1-inch chunks
5 fresh mint leaves
2 cups buttermilk
2 cups chicken stock
1 tablespoon lime juice
½ teaspoon salt
8 mint leaves for garnish

1. Place the cucumbers and mint in a blender or food processor and whirl to a fine puree. Pour the puree into a 2-quart pitcher. Add the buttermilk, chicken stock, lime juice, and salt and mix well.

2. Chill the soup for at least 1 hour until it is icy cold then pour into thermos bottles. Put the mint leaves in a small plastic bag and at the picnic, garnish each serving with a mint leaf.

LEMONY CHICKEN
▼▼▼▼▼▼▼▼▼▼▼▼▼

Serves 8   Preparation Time: 1 hour   Marinating Time: 12 hours   Baking Time: 35 to 40 minutes

12 to 16 chicken thighs, with skin removed
1 cup lemon juice
1 cup all-purpose flour
½ teaspoon salt
freshly ground black pepper
¼ teaspoon dried thyme
2 tablespoons corn oil
2 tablespoons butter
½ cup chicken stock
2 tablespoons lemon juice
1 tablespoon grated lemon rind
¼ teaspoon dried thyme

1. Rinse the chicken in cold water and pat dry. Place in a low-sided baking dish and cover with the 1 cup of lemon juice. Marinate in the refrigerator for about 12 hours, turning several times. Let the chicken sit at room temperature for 30 minutes before cooking.

2. Put the flour, salt, pepper, and thyme in a medium-size paper bag and shake a few pieces of chicken at a time in the bag until they are evenly coated in the flour mixture.

3. Meanwhile, heat the oil and butter until hot, but not smoking over medium heat in a large skillet. Add enough chicken thighs to cover the bottom of the skillet without crowding, and sauté for about 5 to 10 minutes on each side or until the pieces are golden brown. Gently remove the chicken from the skillet and place in a large low-sided baking dish.

4. Preheat the oven to 350° F.

5. Mix the stock with the 2 tablespoons of lemon juice and pour it around the chicken in the baking dish. Sprinkle each piece with a little of the lemon rind and thyme. Bake for 35 to 40 minutes or until the chicken is cooked through, but not dry, or cook the chicken in a microwave oven according to oven directions. Place the pan uncovered in the refrigerator to cool. When cool, arrange the chicken on two lightweight picnic serving plates and cover them tightly with plastic wrap. Refrigerate until cold. Pack the plates in an insulated bag with a frozen ice pack.

RED POTATO SALAD WITH FRESH PEAS
▼▼▼▼▼▼▼▼▼▼▼▼▼

Serves 8   Preparation Time: 30 minutes

2 pounds small red potatoes, washed and cut into halves or quarters (about 8 cups — leave the skins on)
1 medium videlia or sweet onion, chopped
¼ cup cider vinegar
½ teaspoon salt
2 tablespoons mayonnaise
1 tablespoon Dijon mustard
¼ cup plain yogurt
freshly ground black pepper
4 leaves frest mint, chopped,
or 1 tablespoon minced fresh dill
1 pound fresh peas, shelled

1. Bring a large pot of salted water to a boil. Add the potatoes and cook for 15 minutes or until the potatoes are tender when pierced with a sharp knife. Drain the potatoes and place them in a large bowl with the onions, 2 tablespoons of the vinegar, and the salt. Gently stir the potatoes to combine all the ingredients. Cover the bowl with plastic wrap and let it sit unrefrigerated for 30 minutes to blend the flavors.

2. In a small bowl, whisk together the remaining vinegar, mayonnaise, mustard, yogurt, and pepper just until smooth. Pour this dressing over the marinated potatoes and stir to blend. Sprinkle the mint or dill over the salad and scatter the peas over all. Store the salad in two covered 1-quart containers and chill until ready to pack in an insulated bag for the picnic.

TANNIES

▼▼▼▼▼▼▼▼▼▼▼▼▼

Serves 8   Preparation Time: 10 minutes   Baking Time: 35 minutes

20 graham crackers, rolled into crumbs
½ cup wheat germ
one 14-ounce can evaporated milk
one 6-ounce package chocolate chips
1 teaspoon pure vanilla extract
½ cup chopped walnuts (optional)

1. Preheat the oven to 350° F.

2. Combine the graham cracker crumbs, wheat germ, milk, chocolate chips, vanilla, and nuts in a large bowl and mix well.

3. Spread the batter in a greased 9-inch-by-9-inch square baking pan and bake for 35 minutes or until lightly browned on top. Cool the tannies in the pan for 5 minutes only, then cut into squares and remove from the pan. Cool completely on wire racks. Pack the tannies in a seal-lock plastic bag and place on the top of the pack when it is time to travel.

WHITE WINE SPRITZERS
▼▼▼▼▼▼▼▼▼▼▼▼▼

Serves 8 generously   *Preparation Time: 5 minutes*

one 1.5 liter bottle good white wine, chilled
one 1 liter bottle sparkling water, chilled
1 lemon, thinly sliced

Fill each glass almost half full of wine, top off with the sparkling water, and add a twist of lemon.

SPARKLING CRANBERRY JUICE
▼▼▼▼▼▼▼▼▼▼▼▼▼

Serves 8 generously   *Preparation Time: 5 minutes*

one 48-ounce bottle cranberry juice cocktail, chilled
one 1 liter bottle sparkling water, chilled
1 lemon, thinly sliced

Fill each glass almost half full of cranberry juice, top off with the sparkling water, and add a twist of lemon.

BERRY-PICKING PICNIC

There are those who enjoy picking a berry or two on a nice day and there are those who become compulsive about it. Being of the latter sort, I feel obliged to find ways to make the outing enjoyable for others. This isn't difficult when we pick a sunny Sunday in the height of summer, pack a picnic, beach chairs, and the Sunday paper.

Most berry patches that I know require at least a short hike. This picnic offers a variety of activities and appeals to all ages and dispositions, providing the hike is not too strenuous for the very young or the nonathletic. When you arrive at the chosen spot with a bit of shade and lots of sun, the pickers head for the berry patch and the others stretch out leisurely to read the paper or snooze.

MENU

COLD BERRY SOUP*

PRIMAVERA BREAD*

ASSORTED CHEESES AND SALAMI

BLUEBERRY-PEACH TART*

CHILLED FRUIT JUICES OR SPARKLING WATER OR CHILLED CHARDONNAY

WINE SUGGESTIONS:

An ultrafine California Chardonnay from Edna Valley or Alderbrook or

a Rosemount Vineyards Australian Semillon-Chardonnay

EXTRA ITEMS TO BRING:

CONTAINERS FOR BERRIES

EXTRA SMALL PLATES FOR DESSERT

SERVING PLATE FOR CHEESES AND MEATS

A BOUQUET OF WILD FLOWERS

INSULATED BAG

BEACH CHAIRS

COLD BERRY SOUP
▼▼▼▼▼▼▼▼▼▼▼▼▼▼

Serves 8   Preparation Time: 10 minutes

3 cups orange juice
3 cups buttermilk
1 tablespoon honey
1 tablespoon lemon juice
dash ground cinnamon
dash ground nutmeg
1 cup washed fresh berries
(blueberries, strawberries, raspberries, blackberries or any combination)

1. Whisk together the orange juice, buttermilk, honey, lemon juice, cinnamon, and nutmeg in a large bowl and chill the soup thoroughly.

2. Pour into a large thermos bottle and put in your pack. Place the berries in a seal-lock plastic bag and put in the pack. Serve the soup in cups and divide the berries among the cups.

PRIMAVERA BREAD
▼▼▼▼▼▼▼▼▼▼▼▼▼

Makes 1 loaf　　　*Preparation Time: 1 hour*　　　*Rising Time: 2 hours*　　　*Baking Time: 30 to 40 minutes*

1 cup warm water
1 tablespoon active dry yeast
½ teaspoon salt
1 tablespoon sugar
1 egg, slightly beaten
⅓ cup powdered milk
4½ cups unbleached all-purpose flour
2 tablespoons minced dried onions
⅓ cup wheat germ
1 tablespoon olive oil
1 tablespoon butter
1 cup finely chopped zucchini
½ cup finely chopped carrots
1 small red bell pepper, finely chopped
1 teaspoon dried basil,
or 2 tablespoons finely chopped fresh basil
½ teaspoon dried thyme
freshly ground black pepper
3 ounces grated sharp cheddar cheese
1 yolk mixed with 1 tablespoon water for glaze

1. In a large bowl, combine the water and yeast. Let the mixture sit for 5 minutes until the yeast is dissolved. Stir in the salt, sugar, egg, powdered milk, and 1 cup of the flour and let the sponge sit for 30 minutes. Add the onions and wheat germ.

2. Meanwhile, heat the oil in a large skillet and sauté the zucchini, carrots, and pepper until crisp tender. Toss the vegetables with the basil, thyme, and lots of pepper. Add these vegetables with the oil to the reserved sponge and mix well. Add the cheese.

3. Add the remaining flour and mix well with a wooden spoon. Place the dough on a well-floured surface and knead for 10 minutes, adding more flour if necessary to prevent stickiness. Return the dough to the large bowl and let it rise for 1 hour or until doubled in bulk.

4. Punch down the dough and place it in a 2-quart round, greased casserole dish and let it rise for another hour, or until it mounds over the top of the dish. With a sharp knife, make three diagonal slashes across the top of the loaf. Brush the bread with the glaze.

5. Preheat the oven to 400° F.

6. Bake the loaf for 30 to 40 minutes or until golden brown on top. Remove the loaf from the dish and cool completely on a wire rack. When cool, slice the bread, pack it in a plastic bag, and arrange it on the top of the picnic pack.

BLUEBERRY-PEACH TART
▼▼▼▼▼▼▼▼▼▼▼▼▼

Makes one 9-inch tart   Preparation Time: 1 hour   Baking Time: 15 to 20 minutes

Crust:
1 cup all-purpose flour
2 tablespoons sugar
5 tablespoons butter or margarine, cut into 1-inch chunks
1 egg, beaten
½ teaspoon pure almond extract
½ cup finely chopped pecans

Filling:
Peach layer
3 cups peeled and sliced fresh peaches
1 teaspoon cornstarch
2 tablespoons sugar
1 tablespoon lemon juice
1 tablespoon butter

Blueberry layer
4 cups blueberries
¼ cup sugar
1 tablespoon cornstarch
dash ground cinnamon
1 teaspoon lemon juice
1 tablespoon butter

1. To make the crust, place the flour and sugar in a food processor. Process briefly to mix. Drop the chunks of butter or margarine into the feed tube with the motor running and process quickly until the mixture is crumbly. Add the egg, almond extract, and pecans and process until just combined. Do not overmix the crust.

2. Form the dough into a flattened ball and press it into the bottom and sides of a 9-inch tart pan with a removable bottom. Chill the crust for 30 minutes.

3. Preheat the oven to 350° F.

4. Bake the crust for 15 to 20 minutes or until slightly brown on the rim. Cool the crust on a wire rack.

5. Meanwhile, make the peach layer by mashing the peaches together with the cornstarch, sugar, and lemon juice in a medium saucepan and cooking them over medium heat for 5 minutes, or until the mixture thickens. Add the butter and stir until blended. Cool slightly and pour into the cooled crust.

6. To make the blueberry layer, mash 2 cups of the blueberries with the sugar, cornstarch, cinnamon, and lemon juice and cook in a large saucepan over medium heat for about 10 minutes or until thickened and translucent. Stir in the butter and the remaining whole blueberries. Cover the peach layer with this blueberry mixture. Leave the tart in the pan and cover tightly with plastic wrap before putting in the pack.

WORKDAY PICNICS

▼▼

Lunches that we bring to work can be boring. In this section are some suggestions for perking up the brown bag. Busy people are apt to take lunch on the run, at their desk, or in some cases, skip it all together. Treat yourself and be good to your body by taking some time for lunch and eating a substantial one. Having a good lunch, and incidentally also a good breakfast, carries you through a long workday and prevents the late afternoon munchies.

How do you turn a bag lunch at your desk into a picnic? You invite some co-workers to join you on a park bench on a beautiful spring day, or sit by a window near a green, leafy plant on a cold winter day. If you're lucky, you will find a nearby picnic table. Picnics are a state of mind. Break up the routine and make a picnic out of your workday lunch.

SPRING LUNCH PICNIC

"Make homemade cake and bread for my lunch? That's too much work," you might say to yourself. Baking does take time, which many only devote to holidays, if at all. However, here is a chance to not only provide some lunch treats for yourself and your family members, but to share some goodies with your fellow workers. In planning an office picnic, to which everyone brings their own lunch, you can offer some delicious homemade cake or bread as a treat for all.

Making bread also takes time and inclination but is worth the effort. This tasty and healthy whole-wheat bread is substantial and yet not dry or heavy. It freezes beautifully as do all types of bread when doubly wrapped. You are in charge of the bread you bake and can control the time spent on it. For example, if you want a very slow rising time, cover the bowl with plastic and place it in the refrigerator for about twenty-four hours. If you want to bake the bread in several days, freeze the dough either before it has risen or afterward. One needn't be a slave to bread dough. If making bread holds no interest for you, find a bakery that makes a good, light whole-wheat bread to substitute.

MENU
FRESH PEA SOUP*

THINLY SLICED TURKEY BREAST SANDWICH WITH GUACAMOLE* ON HONEY WHOLE-WHEAT BREAD*

BUNDT CAKE*

CHILLED GREEN GRAPES

COFFEE, TEA, OR SKIMMED MILK

FRESH PEA SOUP
▼▼▼▼▼▼▼▼▼▼▼▼▼

Homemade soup may not seem to fit into a busy work schedule, but this one is quick and easy as well as delicious.

Serves 4   Preparation Time: 15 minutes

one 10-ounce package frozen peas
(fresh, if available)
1 cup chicken stock (homemade, if available)
1 small onion, chopped
1 teaspoon butter
1 tablespoon lime juice
¼ teaspoon ground nutmeg
1 cup plain yogurt

1. Cook the peas in ¼ cup water in either a microwave oven or a medium-size saucepan following package directions.

2. Heat the chicken stock in a microwave oven, then place it in a blender. Add the peas and cooking liquid and let the mixture sit for 5 minutes.

3. Meanwhile, sauté the onions in the butter for 3 minutes or until soft. Add the onion mixture, lime juice, and nutmeg to the peas and puree until smooth.

4. Add the yogurt and blend briefly. Pour the soup into four 1-cup covered containers and chill until ready to pack one of them in your lunch bag.

GUACAMOLE
▼▼▼▼▼▼▼▼▼▼▼▼▼

Makes 1 cup   Preparation Time: 15 minutes

*1 ripe avocado, preferably
the Haas type with dark bumpy skin
1 medium tomato, chopped with seeds and juice removed
juice of 1 lime
1 teaspoon hot sauce
2 tablespoons minced onions*

1. Cut the avocado in half and remove the pit. Using a spoon, scoop the flesh out of the skin and place it in a medium-size bowl. Mash the avocado with the back of a fork until it is smooth.

2. Add the tomato, lime juice, hot sauce, and onions to the avocado and mix well. Place the guacamole in a covered container and refrigerate until ready to use.

HONEY WHOLE-WHEAT BREAD
▼▼▼▼▼▼▼▼▼▼▼▼▼

This delicious, nutritious bread has been well loved by classes of junior high students for years.

Makes 2 loaves   *Preparation Time: 30 minutes*   *Rising Time: 2 hours*   *Baking Time: 40 to 50 minutes*

2½ cups warm water
2 tablespoons active dry yeast
1 teaspoon salt
¼ cup softened margarine
¼ cup honey
⅓ cup powdered milk
2½ cups all-purpose flour
4 to 5 cups whole-wheat flour

1. Place the water and yeast in a large bowl and let the mixture sit for 5 minutes until the yeast is dissolved.

2. Meanwhile, in a small bowl, mix the salt, margarine, honey, and powdered milk into a paste. Add this to the yeast mixture and blend well with a large whisk.

3. Add the all-purpose flour and beat with the whisk or a wooden spoon until the flour is well blended. Gradually add the whole-wheat flour, one cup at a time, and continue beating with a wooden spoon. When the dough seems to come together in a ball in the center of the bowl and is soft, but not sticky, scrape the sides of the bowl and dump all the contents on a lightly floured surface. At this point, you will not have added all the whole-wheat flour.

4. Knead the dough for about 10 minutes. As it gets sticky, add small amounts of the remaining whole-wheat flour. When the dough is well kneaded, it will have absorbed most of the flour and will be smooth and round and softly firm to the touch. It should not be sticky (too little flour), or rigid (too much flour).

5. Put the dough into a clean, oiled bowl, turn the dough over to coat it with oil, cover it with a damp cloth, and let it rise in a warm, draft-free place until it is double in bulk, about 45 minutes to 1 hour.

6. When the dough has risen according to your schedule, punch it down and knead it two times to form a smooth shape and to release the air bubbles. Divide the dough into two equal pieces and shape each one into a loaf. Place the loaves in 9-inch by 4-inch by 5-inch loaf pans and cover with a clean dish towel. Let the loaves rise for 1 hour or until doubled in size again.

7. While the dough is rising, preheat the oven to 400° F.

Bake the loaves for 40 to 50 minutes or until brown on top. Remove them from the pans immediately and cool on wire racks. When completely cool, store the loaves in plastic bags.

Note: While it is tempting to taste bread when it is hot from the oven, you will find that it is much easier to slice when slightly cool. Storing bread in the refrigerator dries it out and speeds up the staling process. Bread that you will not eat in a few days is best stored in the freezer. You can quickly thaw it in a microwave oven.

BUNDT CAKE
▼▼▼▼▼▼▼▼▼▼▼▼

Serves 8   Preparation Time: 35 minutes   Baking Time: 60 to 70 minutes

1¾ cups sugar
1 cup butter
1 cup plain yogurt
3 eggs
1 teaspoon pure vanilla extract
2 teaspoons grated lemon rind
2¼ cups all-purpose flour
½ teaspoon salt
½ teaspoon baking soda

1. Preheat the oven to 325° F.

2. In the large bowl of an electric mixer, cream together the sugar and butter until the mixture is light and fluffy. Add the yogurt, eggs, vanilla, and lemon rind. Continue beating until the mixture is well blended.

3. Sift the flour, salt, and baking soda into a medium-size bowl and gradually add the flour mixture to the egg mixture with the mixer running at low speed. Beat the batter for 3 minutes until light colored.

4. Pour the batter into a greased and floured bundt pan and bake for 60 to 70 minutes or until lightly browned on top, and a tester inserted in the center comes out clean.

5. Cool upright on a wire rack for 15 minutes. Remove the cake from the pan and cool completely on a wire rack.

WINTER LUNCH PICNIC

A picnic at work offers a pleasant interlude in a busy schedule. Not all offices are suited to picnics, but be creative about introducing the concept to your colleagues. Find a window where the winter sun can enter, grab a plant or two, and encourage everyone to share their bag lunches.

MENU

PICNIC CALZONES*

COLD ZUCCHINI AND TOMATOES*

PRIZE WINNING CHOCOLATE CHIP COOKIES*

NATURAL SODA OR HOT HERBAL TEA

EXTRA ITEMS TO BRING:

PLANTS, OR A BOUQUET OF FLOWERS

A BRIGHT TABLECLOTH

SUNSHINE

PICNIC CALZONES
▼▼▼▼▼▼▼▼▼▼▼▼▼

These pastries could be called pocket pizzas. Start with a simple yeast dough, fill it with your favorite pizza filling, and wrap it up in a neat little package.

Serves 6   Preparation Time: 30 minutes   Rising Time: 1 hour   Baking Time: 15 to 20 minutes

1 tablespoon active dry yeast
1 cup warm water
1 tablespoon honey
½ teaspoon salt
2½ to 3 cups all-purpose flour

FILLING:
Fill the calzones with whatever you love!
Here are some suggestions that you can use in combination.

one 10-ounce package frozen spinach, steamed and well drained by pressing through a sieve
ricotta cheese
grated mozzarella cheese
grated Parmesan cheese
sautéed chopped onions and garlic
tomato sauce

1. In a large bowl, place the yeast, water, honey, and salt. Stir with a wooden spoon until the yeast has dissolved.

2. Add 2 cups of the flour and beat the mixture with the wooden spoon until it is smooth. Gradually add the remaining flour and continue to stir with the wooden spoon, until the dough forms a ball.

3. Scrape the dough out of the bowl and place on a lightly floured surface and knead the dough until it is smooth and elastic. Add more flour if the dough becomes sticky.

4. Place the dough in a lightly greased bowl and cover it with a damp towel. Let the dough rise in a warm spot for 1 hour or until double in bulk. Punch down the dough. At this point, the dough is ready to be shaped. If that is not possible, store in the freezer.

5. Preheat the oven to 450° F.

6. Divide the dough into six equal parts. Roll each piece into a ¼-inch thick round that is about six inches in diameter. With a finger, moisten a half-inch around the edge of each piece with water.

7. Place 2 to 3 tablespoons of filling on each round, slightly off center. Fold the empty side over the filling and crimp with a fork. Prick holes in the top.

8. Bake for 15 to 20 minutes or until lightly browned.

COLD ZUCCHINI AND TOMATOES
▼▼▼▼▼▼▼▼▼▼▼▼▼

This vegetable dish is almost like a relish and can be served as such. It goes well with grilled meats and chicken.

Serves 8   Preparation Time: 30 minutes   Chilling Time: 1 hour

¼ cup olive oil
2 tablespoons vegetable oil
2 large onions, thinly sliced
3 or 4 small zucchini, sliced
1½ pounds tomatoes, seeded and cut into bite-size chunks,
or one 28-ounce can Italian tomatoes
4 leaves fresh basil, chopped, or 1 tablespoon dried basil
½ teaspoon dried oregano
½ teaspoon salt
freshly ground black pepper

1. Heat the oils in a large skillet, add the onions and cook 5 minutes over medium heat until slightly soft. Add the zucchini, cover the skillet, and cook 10 minutes more. Uncover, add the tomatoes, basil, oregano, salt, and pepper, and cook 10 minutes, stirring frequently.

2. Pour the vegetables into a dish and chill for at least 1 hour or until very cold. Pack some in a container and put it in your lunch bag.

PRIZE WINNING CHOCOLATE CHIP COOKIES
▼▼▼▼▼▼▼▼▼▼▼▼▼

(from The Search for the Perfect Chocolate Chip Cookie *by Gwen Steege, Storey Publishing, 1988)*

Makes 3 dozen   Preparation Time: 45 minutes   Baking Time: 12 to 13 minutes

1 ¾ cups all-purpose flour
¼ teaspoon baking soda
1 cup softened butter or margarine
1 teaspoon pure vanilla extract
1 cup granulated sugar
½ cup firmly packed dark brown sugar
1 egg
⅓ cup unsweetened cocoa
2 tablespoons milk
1 cup chopped pecans or walnuts
1 cup semisweet chocolate chips

1. Preheat the oven to 350° F.

2. Combine the flour and baking soda in a medium-size bowl and set aside.

3. In the large bowl of an electric mixer, cream the butter at high speed. Add the vanilla and sugars and beat until fluffy. Beat in the egg. At low speed, beat in the cocoa, then the milk.

4. Stir in the reserved dry ingredients with a wooden spoon and mix until just blended. Add the nuts and chocolate chips and stir to combine.

5. Drop the dough by rounded teaspoonsful onto a nonstick or foil-lined baking sheet. Bake for 12 to 13 minutes or until set. Remove the cookies from the oven and cool on wire racks for two minutes before removing them from the baking sheet. Cool cookies completely on wire racks and pack in a seal-lock plastic bag for traveling in your lunch bag.

POTLUCK PICNICS

▼▼

Picnics are often gatherings where each participant or family contributes to the spread of food. Historically that was what was meant by a picnic. Today we call this a potluck picnic, although at times it is far from a random "potluck" selection. Writing in the late nineteenth century, the much admired and quoted French gastronome, Brillat-Savarin, describes how the outdoors enhances the lively appreciation of good food when he writes of picnickers, "Seating themselves on the green sward they eat while the corks fly and there is talk, laughter and merriment, and perfect freedom, for the universe is their drawing room and the sun their lamp. Besides, they have appetite, nature's special gift, which lends to such a meal a vivacity unknown indoors, however beautiful the surroundings."

Frequently when friends or family gather for a picnic, the meal is orchestrated around one special dish which is provided by the planner of the picnic and the guests bring the rest. This is a great way to entertain because you can devote your energy to the special dish and the organization of the picnic without spending hours cooking You can be very precise and give out the recipes, as my totally take-charge friend does, or you can ask people to bring a certain type of food, such as a salad. One way of organizing a potluck picnic is to give no guidance and just ask people to bring a favorite food. Amazingly, this method usually produces a most interesting array of food that is usually quite diverse. One runs the risk of having all desserts, but that would not be a total disaster, would it?

This chapter contains menus designed for the shared meal.

FAMILY CELEBRATION PICNIC IN THE BACKYARD

Summer is often the time when families gather together to share a vacation spot or a day together. When the clan gathers to celebrate a special occasion, everyone can bring something to contribute to the meal. Depending on the size of your family, this could be either a small or a very large party. The recipes in this chapter are generally made to serve eight people. If you are serving a large crowd, have several people make the same dish or have them make a double batch.

MENU

TACO SALAD*

BARBECUED CHICKEN*

EIGHT BEAN SALAD*

CORN ON THE COB AND GARDEN LETTUCE TOSSED SALAD

GRAMMA BEA'S STRAWBERRY SHORTCAKE*

ICED TEA OR COLD BEER OR CHILLED WHITE WINE

BEER AND WINE SUGGESTIONS:

Anchor Steam Beer from San Francisco, Samuel Adams Beer,

or Pilsner Urquel; Alsacian Pinot Blanc or California Sauvignon Blanc

EXTRA ITEMS TO BRING:

LARGE BOUQUET OF SUMMER FLOWERS

CROQUET

BADMINTON

PADDLE BALL

TACO SALAD
▼▼▼▼▼▼▼▼▼▼▼▼▼▼

This is called a salad but is really a hearty appetizer. In essence, it is a dip with several layers. Use your imagination to add more layers.

Serves 8   *Preparation Time: 30 minutes*

one 15-ounce can refried beans (optional)
1½ cups grated cheddar or Monterey Jack cheese (optional)
1 cup Guacamole (see recipe page 50)
½ cup medium salsa
½ cup plain yogurt
2 medium tomatoes, chopped and seeded
6 green onions, chopped, including at least 1 inch of the green tops
1 large bag nacho chips

1. In a 10-inch deep-dish nonmetal pie pan (preferably a decorative one), spread the beans evenly over the bottom. Sprinkle the cheese over the beans. Place in a microwave oven for 30 seconds on high until the cheese melts.

2. Spread the guacamole over the cheese, then a thin layer of the salsa. Gently spread the yogurt over the salsa.

3. Arrange the tomatoes in a ring around the outer edge of the pie pan. Make an inner ring by sprinkling the green onions inside the ring of tomatoes.

4. Place the chips in a large basket and watch this appetizer disappear before your eyes.

Note: For a less filling appetizer, omit the layer of beans and cheese.

BARBECUED CHICKEN
▼▼▼▼▼▼▼▼▼▼▼▼▼

Serves 8   Preparation Time: 2 hours   Cooking Time: 40 to 50 minutes

2 broiling chickens, cut into quarters, or 8 chicken breast halves

SAUCE:
¼ cup packed brown sugar
¼ cup Dijon mustard
¾ cup cider vinegar
½ cup pineapple or orange juice
¼ cup Worchestershire sauce
½ teaspoon Tabasco sauce

1. Wash chicken pieces in cold water and pat dry. Place in a large, low-sided glass baking dish and refrigerate while you make the sauce.

2. Place all the ingredients for the sauce in a small bowl and whisk together until well blended.

3. Pour the sauce over the chicken and turn each piece so it is coated with barbecue sauce. Cover the pan with plastic wrap and refrigerate for several hours. Remove the chicken from the refrigerator an hour before cooking, turn the pieces again, and let them sit out at room temperature.

4. Preheat a gas grill or build a charcoal fire while the chicken sits at room temperature. Turn the gas grill to low or spread out the coals to provide a low even heat. Remove the chicken from the dish and place the pieces on the grill. With a pastry brush, brush each piece with the barbecue sauce and reserve the remaining sauce. Turn each piece and brush again. Close the lid of the gas grill and cook the chicken for 50 to 60 minutes or until crusty and tender. Brush with the sauce every 15 minutes. If you are cooking the chicken on charcoal, you must watch it carefully and turn it often so it doesn't burn. The gas grill is highly recommended because the heat is controlled and the chicken remains tender and moist.

5. Remove the chicken from the grill and place on a serving dish.

6. If the chicken is going to travel, let it cool slightly and then refrigerate it until cold. Wrap the cold chicken in aluminum foil until ready to pack the picnic. If you are not traveling far, the chicken can be packed in a basket. However, if it will be several hours before you eat, it is best to pack the chicken in the cooler.

Note: To avoid blackened chicken on an open grill, pre-cook the chicken in a microwave or conventional oven and merely brown it on the grill. However, the slow cooking in a covered grill makes a wonderfully moist piece of chicken without burning the outside.

EIGHT BEAN SALAD
▼▼▼▼▼▼▼▼▼▼▼▼▼

This salad uses a mix of beans similar to the Ten Bean Soup on page 26. You can buy the dried beans in quantity and make up packages of them for soup and salad. They make great hostess gifts, too, if you tie on a tag with the recipe. A timesaving alternative is to use whatever canned beans are available in your local market.

Serves 8   Preparation Time for dried beans: Overnight
Cooking Time for dried beans: 1 hour   Preparation Time for salad: 30 minutes

2 cups mixed dried beans
(¼ cup each of garbanzo, navy, red kidney, lima, pinto, black-eyed peas, and split peas)
4 quarts water, divided
½ pound fresh green beans, trimmed and cut into 1-inch pieces
½ pound fresh wax beans, trimmed and cut into 1-inch pieces
8 green onions, coarsely chopped with green tops
½ cup finely chopped fresh parsley

VINAIGRETTE:
¼ cup white wine vinegar
1 tablespoon sugar
3 large garlic cloves, minced
1 teaspoon dry mustard
¼ teaspoon salt
freshly ground black pepper
½ cup corn oil
¼ cup olive oil

1. Place the dried beans in a large saucepan and cover with water. Let the beans soak overnight or for several hours. Drain the beans and rinse with cold water. Put them back in the saucepan and add 2 quarts of the water. Over high heat, bring the water to a boil. Reduce the heat, cover the pot, and simmer the beans for 1 hour or until tender. Remove from the heat, drain, rinse, and chill them in a large bowl. If you use canned beans, merely drain and rinse them. You should have 4 cups of drained beans.

2. Place the remaining 2 quarts of water in a large saucepan and over high heat, bring to a rapid boil. Add the prepared green beans and wax beans. When the water begins to boil again, cook the beans for 2 minutes or until crunchy tender. Remove the beans from the heat and drain. Plunge them quickly into ice water to stop the cooking. Drain thoroughly and add them to the cooked dried beans.

3. Add the green onions and parsley to the beans and gently mix.

4. To make the vinaigrette, place the vinegar, sugar, garlic, mustard, salt, and several gratings of pepper into a blender or food processor. Blend the mixture well. Slowly drizzle the oils into the mixture with the motor running and continue blending until you have a thick, creamy vinaigrette.

5. Pour the vinaigrette over the beans, place in a serving bowl, cover with plastic wrap, and chill. If this salad is to be part of a movable feast, place it in a 2-quart container with a lid and refrigerate until travel time. It does not need to be kept cold while traveling.

GRAMMA BEA'S STRAWBERRY SHORTCAKE
▼▼▼▼▼▼▼▼▼▼▼▼▼

Serves 8   Preparation Time: 45 minutes   Baking Time: 10 to 12 minutes

SHORTCAKE:
2 cups all-purpose flour
¼ teaspoon salt
4 teaspoons baking powder
2 tablespoons sugar
¼ cup very cold butter
1 egg, well beaten
⅓ cup light cream

STRAWBERRY FILLING:
3 quarts fresh, unhulled, unwashed strawberries
4 tablespoons sugar

WHIPPED CREAM:
2 cups heavy cream
2 tablespoons Grand Marnier liqueur, or 2 teaspoons pure vanilla extract

SHORTCAKE:

1. Preheat the oven to 450° F.

2. Place the dry ingredients in a food processor. With the steel blade, process briefly. Add the butter to the flour mixture and process until it resembles coarse crumbs.

3. Mix the egg and cream together in a small bowl and pour into the flour mixture with the motor running. Process until the dough forms a ball.

4. Place the dough on a lightly floured surface and knead about 10 times. Pat or roll the dough to a ½-inch thickness.

5. With a 2½-inch round cookie cutter, cut the dough into rounds and place them on an ungreased baking sheet.

6. Bake the shortcakes for 10 to 12 minutes or until golden brown. Remove from the baking sheet and cool on a wire rack. When cool, slice the shortcakes in half horizontally, but keep each one intact. Stack them in two layers and wrap them together in aluminum foil. Pack the shortcakes on the top of the picnic basket. The shortcakes could be made well in advance of the picnic and stored in the freezer until the day of the picnic. Just be sure they are thawed before serving.

STRAWBERRY FILLING:

1. To prepare the strawberries on the day of the picnic, place them in a colander and quickly wash them in cold water. Reserve eight of the best looking berries and remove the hulls from the rest. Cut the large berries in half or quarters so all the pieces are approximately the same size. Place the hulled berries in a 2-quart container with a lid and sprinkle the sugar over them to draw out the juices. Cover the berries and store in the refrigerator until you pack the basket. Place the eight select berries in a plastic sandwich bag.

WHIPPED CREAM:

1. Just before leaving for the picnic, place the cream in the medium-size bowl of an electric mixer and whip at high speed until soft peaks form. Stir in the Grand Marnier or vanilla. Mound the whipped cream in a container with a tight-fitting lid and pack in a cooler.

When it is time to present this creation, place a shortcake bottom in each bowl and cover with a generous amount of berries. Place a large dollop of whipped cream on top of the berries and cover with the shortcake top. Divide the remaining berries among the eight servings, add a little more whipped cream, place a select strawberry on top of each, and serve.

NEIGHBORHOOD POOLSIDE PICNIC

When I was growing up, the neighbors shared the work and pleasure of digging and building a swimming pool from scratch. The result was that every summer weekend we shared meals by the pool. Usually a large piece of meat was communally purchased (before the days of cholesterol watching) and grilled. Each family contributed salads, desserts, and appetizers which were shared. This is a modern version of our poolside picnics.

MENU

HUMMUS* WITH WHOLE-WHEAT OR PLAIN PITA BREAD

GRILLED SALMON FILLETS WITH MUSTARD DILL SAUCE*

ARTICHOKE SALAD*

VONNIE'S FROSTY FRUIT SALAD*

BUTTER LETTUCE WITH LEMON VINAIGRETTE

CRUSTY FRENCH BREAD WITH GARLIC BUTTER

CHOCOLATE ZUCCHINI CAKE* OR CHOCOLATE LUSH*

CHILLED WHITE ZINFANDEL

WINE SUGGESTIONS:

Glen Ellen or Sutter Home White Zinfandel on the slightly sweet side or Beringer, Deloach, or

Beuhler White Zinfandel for those whose taste runs to dry

EXTRA ITEMS TO BRING:

MANY BEACH TOWELS

POOL TOYS AND RAFTS

INFLATED BALLS

BASKETS OF FLOWERS

HUMMUS
▼▼▼▼▼▼▼▼▼▼▼▼▼

Makes 3 cups   Preparation Time: 15 minutes

2 cups slightly drained cooked garbanzo beans
3 to 4 garlic cloves, minced
½ teaspoon tamari
¼ cup lemon juice
¾ cup sesame tahini
freshly ground black pepper
1 package whole-wheat pita bread
1 package plain pita bread

1. Place the beans, garlic, tamari, lemon juice, tahini, and a generous amount of black pepper in a blender or food processor and process until smooth and creamy.

2. Place the hummus in a 1-quart covered container. Store in the refrigerator until it's time to pack it in the picnic basket. Hummus also freezes beautifully.

3. Cut the pita bread into 1-inch wedges and place in a plastic bag until packing time. Bring a basket for serving the pita bread.

GRILLED SALMON FILLETS WITH MUSTARD DILL SAUCE
▼▼▼▼▼▼▼▼▼▼▼▼▼

Serves 8   Preparation Time: 20 minutes

4 pounds salmon fillets

SAUCE:
½ cup plain yogurt
2 tablespoons mayonnaise
¼ cup Dijon mustard
1 tablespoon minced fresh dill
1 tablespoon lemon juice
dill sprigs for garnish

1. Rinse the salmon in cold water and remove any visible bones. Place the salmon in a low-sided baking dish skin side down.

2. Combine all of the ingredients for the sauce in a small bowl. Whisk until well blended.

3. Brush the salmon lightly with the sauce and let it reach room temperature while preparing the grill.

4. Preheat the gas grill at high heat and then turn down to low, or build a medium charcoal fire. Grill the salmon for 7 to 10 minutes on a side, or until the flesh is flaky.

5. Arrange the salmon on a serving plate and spoon the remaining sauce over the pieces. Garnish with the dill sprigs.

ARTICHOKE SALAD
▼▼▼▼▼▼▼▼▼▼▼▼▼

Serves 8   Preparation Time: 30 minutes   Marinating Time: Overnight

½ pound fresh mushrooms, washed, dried, and sliced
three 6-ounce jars marinated artichoke hearts with marinade
1 medium tomato, seeded and cut into bite-size chunks
1 stalk celery, sliced
1 small sweet onion, thinly sliced
4 green onions, thinly sliced, including some green tops
6 sun-dried tomatoes, cut into strips

DRESSING:
2 tablespoons balsamic vinegar
1 teaspoon lemon juice
½ teaspoon dried oregano
¼ teaspoon salt
1 teaspoon sugar
freshly ground black pepper
2 tablespoons vegetable oil
2 tablespoons olive oil

1. In a large bowl, combine all of the vegetables. Whisk the dressing ingredients together in a small bowl and pour over the vegetables.

2. Let the salad stand in the refrigerator overnight, or 8 hours. Place in a serving bowl at picnic time.

VONNIE'S FROSTY FRUIT SALAD
▼▼▼▼▼▼▼▼▼▼▼▼▼

The thought of this sweet salad recalls hot summer weekends in the 1950s amidst friends and family of all ages. I couldn't resist adding it to this menu.

Serves 8   Preparation Time: 30 minutes   Chilling Time: 2 to 3 hours

1 tablespoon gelatin
¼ cup cold water
1 egg white, stiffly beaten
½ cup sugar
1 cup heavy cream, whipped
½ cup plain yogurt
1 ½ cups red or green seedless grapes
1 cup drained fresh pineapple
½ cup broken walnuts
curly endive or escarole for garnish

1. Dissolve the gelatin in the cold water. Heat the mixture to a boil in a microwave oven and then slowly pour it over the beaten egg white, while the beater is still running. Gradually add the sugar and continue beating for 5 minutes or until very thick. Cool the mixture in the refrigerator for 15 to 20 minutes.

2. Remove the mixture from the refrigerator and fold in the whipped cream and the remaining ingredients. Pour the salad into a 2-quart mold and chill for 2 to 3 hours.

3. Unmold the salad onto a plate just before bringing to the picnic. Decorate the edges with the endive or escarole.

CHOCOLATE ZUCCHINI CAKE
▼▼▼▼▼▼▼▼▼▼▼▼▼

(from Garden Way's Joy of Gardening Cookbook by Janet Ballantyne, Garden Way Inc., 1984)

Serves 8   Preparation Time: 25 minutes   Baking Time: 40 minutes

4 ounces unsweetened chocolate, melted
½ cup vegetable oil
½ cup softened butter
2 cups sugar
3 eggs, beaten
1 tablespoon pure vanilla extract
2 cups sifted unbleached all-purpose flour
⅓ cup cocoa
2 teaspoons baking soda
2 teaspoons baking powder
1 teaspoon salt
⅓ cup buttermilk
3 cups coarsely grated zucchini
½ cup chopped nuts
1 recipe for Orange Cream Cheese Icing (see page 85)

1. Preheat the oven to 350° F.

2. Combine the chocolate and oil in a small bowl.

3. In a large bowl, cream the butter and sugar until light and fluffy. Add the eggs and vanilla and beat well. Stir in the chocolate mixture until well mixed.

4. Sift the dry ingredients in the batter and add the buttermilk. Stir until the batter is smooth. Mix the zucchini and nuts into the batter.

5. Pour the batter into a 9-inch-by-13-inch rectangular pan and bake for 40 minutes, or until a tester inserted in the center of the cake comes out clean. Cool the cake completely on a wire rack. When cool, frost in the pan with the cream cheese frosting. Cut into serving pieces and bring to the picnic.

CHOCOLATE LUSH
▼▼▼▼▼▼▼▼▼▼▼▼▼

This rich chocolate concoction is in the tradition of the old-fashioned upside-down cake. It was a family favorite and deserves to be revived. It has the added benefit of being a low cholesterol, low-fat chocolate dessert.

Serves 8   Preparation Time: 20 minutes   Baking Time: 45 minutes

1 cup unbleached all-purpose flour
2 teaspoons baking powder
½ teaspoon baking soda
¼ teaspoon salt
½ cup granulated sugar
¼ cup cocoa
2 tablespoons vegetable oil
½ cup milk
1 teaspoon pure vanilla extract
½ cup chopped walnuts (optional)

TOPPING:
½ cup firmly packed light brown sugar
6 tablespoons cocoa
2 tablespoons butter
1½ cups hot water
¼ teaspoon salt

1. Preheat the oven to 350° F.

2. In a large bowl, sift together the flour, baking powder, baking soda, salt, granulated sugar, and cocoa. Combine the oil, milk, and vanilla in a small bowl, stir into the flour mixture, and mix well. Add the chopped walnuts. Spread the batter in a greased 9-inch-by-9-inch baking pan.

3. Whisk the topping ingredients together in a small bowl and pour evenly over the batter. The topping will be very soupy. Bake for 45 minutes, or until the cake comes away from the sides of the pan. Cool in the pan on a wire rack. Cut into squares and serve at the picnic.

APRES SKI PICNIC

After a day on the slopes, try an indoor picnic by the fire. Spread the food on a low table, take off those heavy ski boots, relax and enjoy good food and fellowship. Being warm and cozy inside feels even better as the temperature drops and the wind howls outside.

MENU

SPICY BEANS WITH SAUSAGE*

GREEN BEANS AND TOMATOES*

MEXICAN CORNBREAD*

BROWNIES*

HOT CHOCOLATE OR GLÜ WINE*

EXTRA ITEMS TO BRING:

SWEATPANTS AND SOFT SHOES

SPICY BEANS WITH SAUSAGE
▼▼▼▼▼▼▼▼▼▼▼▼▼

Serves 8   *Soaking Time: Overnight*   *Preparation Time: 1 hour 15 minutes*   *Baking Time: 8 hours*

2 cups dried navy beans, soaked overnight, rinsed, and drained
1 cup dried red kidney beans, soaked overnight, rinsed, and drained
or 6 cups canned beans instead of 3 cups dried
6 cups water
1 bay leaf
1 tablespoon corn oil
1 medium onion, chopped
1 garlic clove, minced
one 10-ounce package frozen corn
5 slices bacon, crisp-cooked, drained, and crumbled
1 medium green pepper, seeded and chopped
2 tablespoons tomato paste
1 tablespoon white vinegar
1 tablespoon brown sugar
1 teaspoon chili powder
½ teaspoon salt
freshly ground black pepper
1 to 2 pounds kielbasa sausage, cut into 1-inch chunks
½ cup grated cheddar cheese

1. Place the navy and kidney beans and bay leaf in a large pot and add the water. Bring to a boil over high heat, then turn down and simmer for 1 hour, or until the beans are tender. Drain the beans and reserve the liquid.

2. Preheat the oven to 250° F.

3. Place the beans and 3 cups of the reserved liquid in a Dutch oven and bake, covered tightly for 8 hours, stirring occasionally. Add more liquid if beans begin to dry out.

4. While the beans are still baking, heat the oil in a medium-size skillet and sauté the onion and garlic for 2 minutes until slightly softened.

5. Remove the beans from the oven. Turn up the oven to 350° F.

6. Add the onion, garlic, corn, bacon, pepper, tomato paste, vinegar, brown sugar, chili powder, salt, and pepper to the beans.

7. Cook the kielbasa in a skillet for about 15 minutes and add it to the beans. Stir to mix and return the beans to the oven for 30 to 40 minutes or until bubbly. Just before serving, sprinkle the cheese over the top.

GREEN BEANS AND TOMATOES
▼▼▼▼▼▼▼▼▼▼▼▼▼

Serves 8   Preparation Time: 30 minutes   Baking Time: 20 minutes

*2 pounds fresh green beans, trimmed and cut into 2-inch pieces,
or two 10-ounce packages frozen green beans
½ cup olive oil
2 large onions, thinly sliced
4 garlic cloves, minced
1½ teaspoons dried basil
¼ cup minced fresh parsley
salt and pepper to taste
one 28-ounce can tomatoes, drained of all but ⅓ cup juice, or
3½ cups chopped tomatoes*

1. Preheat the oven to 350° F.

2. Fill a large saucepan half-full of water and bring to a boil. Parboil the beans for 2 or 3 minutes. Or, partially cook the frozen beans according to the directions on the package. Drain the beans and place in a 2-quart flat casserole dish.

3. In a medium-size skillet, heat the oil over medium heat and sauté the onions and garlic until soft.

4. Add the basil, parsley, salt, pepper, and tomatoes with juice to the onion mixture and mix well. Spoon the onion mixture over the beans. Bake for 20 minutes. Cool the beans completely, cover with plastic wrap, and refrigerate for a day before serving. These beans can be made ahead and served at room temperature.

MEXICAN CORNBREAD
▼▼▼▼▼▼▼▼▼▼▼▼▼

(based on a recipe from *The Moosewood Cookbook* by Mollie Katzen, Ten Speed Press, 1977)

Makes one 8-inch square pan (To serve 8 generously, make 2)   *Preparation Time: 45 minutes*
Baking Time: 25 to 30 minutes

1 cup all-purpose flour
1 cup yellow cornmeal
1 tablespoon baking powder
½ teaspoon salt
1 egg, slightly beaten
1 tablespoon honey
1 cup milk
¼ teaspoon olive oil
1 medium onion, minced
1 cup fresh or frozen whole kernel corn
½ cup grated cheddar cheese

1. Preheat oven to 375° F.

2. In a large bowl, combine the flour, cornmeal, baking powder, and salt.

3. In a small bowl, beat together the egg, honey, and milk.

4. Heat the oil in a small skillet. Add the onion and sauté over medium heat for 5 minutes or until soft.

5. Add the egg mixture to the flour mixture. Mix thoroughly. Add the corn, cheese, and onion mixture, and mix well.

6. Spread the batter in a greased 8-inch-by-8-inch square baking pan. Bake for 25 to 30 minutes or until brown and firm on top. Cool the bread in the pan on a wire rack. When cool, cut into squares.

BROWNIES
▼▼▼▼▼▼▼▼▼▼▼▼▼▼

Don't kid yourself that these are healthy. They are just plain good and very rich with a dense chocolate flavor. To have some leftovers and to allow for snitching, double the recipe.

Makes one 9-inch square pan   *Preparation Time: 20 minutes*   *Baking Time: 35 to 45 minutes*

½ cup softened butter
1½ cups sugar
3 eggs
3 ounces unsweetened chocolate, melted
½ cup all-purpose flour
½ teaspoon salt
½ teaspoon baking powder
1 teaspoon pure almond extract
¾ cup semisweet chocolate chips
¾ cup chopped pecans or walnuts (optional)

1. Preheat oven to 350° F.

2. In a medium-size bowl, cream the butter and sugar together until fluffy. Beat in the eggs, one at a time. Add the melted chocolate and beat well.

3. In a small bowl, sift together the flour, salt, and baking powder. Add the flour mixture to the chocolate mixture and stir to blend. Add the almond extract, chocolate chips, and nuts, and mix well.

4. Pour the batter into a greased 9-inch-by-9-inch square baking pan. Bake for 35 to 45 minutes, or until a tester inserted in the center comes out clean. Cool in the pan on a wire rack. When cool, cut into squares and put on a serving plate.

GLÜ WINE (HOT SPICED WINE)
▼▼▼▼▼▼▼▼▼▼▼▼▼

Serves 8   Preparation Time: 30 minutes

one 1.5 liter bottle burgundy wine
2 oranges, sliced
2 lemons, sliced
5 whole cloves
3 cinnamon sticks
3 whole allspice

1. Place all the ingredients in a heavy kettle. Gently heat the mixture, but do not let it boil. A wood stove is the perfect place to keep this spiced wine hot.

FRIENDS ON A MOUNTAINSIDE PICNIC

An autumn day with crisp air, the smell of dry leaves, and colors at full blaze hits all the senses. Select a mountainside that looks over a valley below, spread your blanket on a level spot, and experience the intensity of the foliage up close and the muted tones on the distant hillsides.

MENU

COLD SLICED MARINATED FLANK STEAK*

TABOULI*

CREAMY HORSERADISH CUCUMBERS*

CRUSTY FRENCH BREAD AND SWEET BUTTER

CARROT CAKE WITH ORANGE CREAM CHEESE ICING*

CHILLED NATURAL FRUIT SODAS OR ICE COLD BEER

EXTRA ITEMS TO BRING:

COOLER

BOUQUET OF FALL FLOWERS

MARINATED FLANK STEAK
▼▼▼▼▼▼▼▼▼▼▼▼▼

Serves 8   Preparation Time: 25 minutes   Marinating Time: 4 hours

one 3½ pound flank steak
⅓ cup corn oil
⅓ cup tamari
1 teaspoon minced fresh gingerroot
1 garlic clove, minced
1 tablespoon lime juice
salt and freshly ground black pepper

1. Rinse the steak in cold water, pat dry, and score the surface with a sharp knife in a crisscross pattern. Place the steak in an oblong baking dish.

2. In a small bowl, mix together the oil, tamari, gingerroot, garlic, and lime juice. Pour the marinade over the flank steak. Turn the steak once to coat both sides. Cover the dish and set it in the refrigerator for 3 hours. Turn the steak several times during that period. Let the steak and marinade sit out of the refrigerator for 1 hour before cooking.

3. Preheat a gas grill to high.

4. Remove the steak from the marinade and place it on the hot grill. Cook it 5 to 7 minutes on a side, depending on the desired doneness.

5. Remove cooked steak from the grill and place it on a platter. Let it sit for several minutes, and then with a large, sharp knife, thinly slice it diagonally to the cutting surface. By slicing it this way, you will get thin strips of steak that are about one and half inches wide.

6. Arrange the slices on a picnic plate and sprinkle them lightly with salt. Grind some pepper over all and drizzle with a little of the remaining marinade. Cover the plate with plastic wrap and store in the refrigerator. Pack the steak in the cooler when ready to go on the picnic.

TABOULI
▼▼▼▼▼▼▼▼▼▼▼▼▼▼

With fresh herbs, tomatoes, and lemon juice blended into a crunchy grain, this salad tastes like summertime.

Serves 8   Preparation Time for grain: 2 hours   Preparation Time for salad: 15 minutes

1 cup bulgar wheat
2 cups water
3 tablespoons olive oil
½ cup cooked, drained, and rinsed garbanzo beans
3 medium tomatoes, chopped and seeded
2 garlic cloves, minced
2 tablespoons chopped fresh chives
2 tablespoons chopped fresh mint leaves
juice of 2 lemons
¼ cup chopped fresh parsley
¼ teaspoon salt
freshly ground black pepper

1. Place the bulgar and water in a large saucepan and bring to a boil. Turn off the heat, cover the pan, and let stand for 1 hour until the bulgar has absorbed all the water.

2. Place the bulgar mixture in a large bowl and toss it with the olive oil. Cover the bowl and place it in the refrigerator for at least 1 hour.

3. Add the remaining ingredients and gently mix the salad together. Place the tabouli in a 1½-quart covered container and store in the refrigerator until ready to pack the picnic. The tabouli does not need to be packed in a cooler.

Note: Leftover tabouli in a pita pocket makes a terrific quick lunch.

CREAMY HORSERADISH CUCUMBERS
▼▼▼▼▼▼▼▼▼▼▼▼▼

Makes 4 cups   *Preparation Time: 15 minutes*   *Chilling Time: 1 hour*

3 cucumbers, peeled and thinly sliced
1 tablespoon salt
1 cup plain yogurt
2 tablespoons cider vinegar
2 teaspoons horseradish
2 tablespoons mayonnaise

1. Spread out the sliced cucumbers in a low, flat baking dish. Sprinkle them with the salt. Cover the dish and chill the cucumbers for 1 hour.

2. Place the cucumbers in a colander and thoroughly rinse. Spread them out on paper towels and pat dry. Extract as much water from the cucumbers as you can. The less water in the cucumber, the creamier the consistency of the salad.

3. In a small bowl, mix the yogurt, vinegar, horseradish, and mayonnaise together until well combined.

4. Place the cucumbers in a 1-quart covered container and pour the yogurt sauce over them. Stir the mixture gently to blend. Store the cucumbers in the refrigerator until you are ready to pack the picnic. Pack the cucumbers in the cooler to keep them cold.

CARROT CAKE WITH ORANGE CREAM CHEESE ICING
▼▼▼▼▼▼▼▼▼▼▼▼▼

Makes 1 cake   Preparation Time: 50 minutes   Baking Time: 35 to 40 minutes

2 cups all-purpose flour
½ teaspoon ground cinnamon
2 teaspoons baking soda
1 ½ cups sugar
1 cup vegetable oil
4 eggs, slightly beaten
1 cup chopped walnuts
½ cup raisins
4 large carrots, peeled and grated

Icing:
8 ounces softened cream cheese
6 tablespoons softened butter
1 pound confectioners' sugar
2 tablespoons grated orange rind
1 tablespoon orange juice

1. Preheat the oven to 325° F.

2. In a large bowl, combine the flour, cinnamon, baking soda, and sugar and stir to blend. Add the oil and eggs and mix well. Stir in the walnuts, raisins, and carrots and continue stirring until the batter is well blended.

3. Place the cake batter into a greased oblong 9-inch-by-13-inch baking pan. Bake for 35 to 40 minutes, or until a tester inserted in the center comes out clean. Cool the cake on a wire rack until completely cool.

4. To make the icing, cream the cheese and butter in a medium-size bowl. Gradually blend in the sugar until well combined. Add the orange rind and juice and mix until smooth.

5. Ice the cooled cake, cover it with plastic wrap, and store in the refrigerator until it is time to pack it in the picnic basket.

REUNION ON AN ISLAND PICNIC

One of my fond memories of living in the San Francisco Bay area is of gathering together all the East Coast friends, the hometown friends we could find, and taking a ferry to Angel Island in the midst of San Francisco Bay for a picnic. Recipes were handed out and everyone contributed an essential ingredient to a wonderful afternoon by the sparkling waters of San Francisco Bay. Find an island and gather old friends together.

MENU

GAZPACHO MADRILEÑO*

BARBECUED BUTTERFLY LAMB*

COLD RICE SALAD* AND CUCUMBER RAITA*

CARROTS WITH MINTED MUSTARD VINAIGRETTE*

SOURDOUGH RYE BREAD AND SWEET BUTTER

ASSORTED FRESH FRUITS AND STRAWBERRY COOKIES*

LEMON ICE WATER OR CALIFORNIA WINES

WINE SUGGESTIONS:

A fine Bordeaux or California Cabernet Sauvignon or a Merlot or a Guigal Côté de Rhone

EXTRA ITEMS TO BRING:

GOOD CARVING KNIFE

PLATTER

CUPS FOR SOUP

CLOTH NAPKINS

WINE GLASSES

FLOWERS

CORKSCREW

TABLECLOTH

A BOWL FOR THE FRUIT

SERVING SPOONS FOR SALADS

CHARCOAL AND MATCHES

HIBACHI, UNLESS THERE IS A GRILL

GAZPACHO MADRILEÑO
▼▼▼▼▼▼▼▼▼▼▼▼▼

A cold Spanish soup made from garden fresh vegetables whets the appetite for what is to follow.

Serves 8   Preparation Time: 15 minutes

1 small green pepper, seeded and cut into chunks
1 medium cucumber, peeled and cut into quarters
1 garlic clove
3 medium-large tomatoes, seeded and cut into chunks
2 tablespoons red wine vinegar
¼ teaspoon ground cumin
½ teaspoon salt
5 tablespoons olive oil
3 cups water

GARNISHES:
1 small green pepper, seeded and chopped
1 small tomato, seeded and chopped
1 small cucumber, peeled and chopped

1. Place the pepper, cucumber, and garlic in a blender or food processor and process briefly. Add the tomatoes, vinegar, cumin, and salt and blend until smooth.

2. Gradually drizzle the oil into the mixture with the motor running and blend until creamy. You have made a concentrate to which you will add the water.

3. Pour the soup into a 1½-quart covered container and refrigerate until ready to pack the picnic.

4. Place the garnishes in individual, small covered containers and chill until ready to go. Serve the soup in cups and let people choose which garnishes they want.

BARBECUED BUTTERFLY LAMB
▼▼▼▼▼▼▼▼▼▼▼▼▼

(from A Private Collection *by the Junior League of Palo Alto, California)*

This is the civilized way to cook a leg of lamb. On one memorable biking picnic, also in California, the entire lamb was splayed on a huge grill placed over an enormous fire. The marinade was applied with a mop. While that was dramatic and fun, this is more manageable and more tasty.

Serves 8   Preparation Time: 20 minutes   Marinating Time: 6 to 8 hours   Cooking Time: 30 to 45 minutes

one 6 to 7 pound leg of lamb, butterflied
1 cup dry red wine
¾ cup beef broth
3 tablespoons orange marmalade
2 tablespoons red wine vinegar
1 tablespoon minced dried onion
1 tablespoon dried marjoram
1 tablespoon dried rosemary
1 large bay leaf, crumbled
1 teaspoon salt
¼ teaspoon ground ginger
1 garlic clove, minced

1. Place the lamb in a shallow roasting pan, fat side down.

2. Combine the remaining ingredients in a large saucepan over medium heat. Simmer, uncovered, for 20 minutes. Pour the hot mixture over the lamb, cover, and let sit for 6 to 8 hours in the refrigerator to marinate. Remove the lamb from the refrigerator 1 hour before cooking. (This can be the time spent traveling to the picnic site.)

3. Prepare a charcoal fire of medium-hot coals. Place the lamb on the grill and cook for 30 to 45 minutes. Turn the meat several times, being careful not to pierce it. Brush the lamb with the marinade as it is cooking.

4. Place the lamb on a platter and slice it thinly on a slight diagonal. Arrange the slices on a plate and put on the picnic table.

COLD RICE SALAD
▼▼▼▼▼▼▼▼▼▼▼▼▼

Serves 8   Preparation Time: 30 minutes

6 cups cooked brown rice
1 medium green pepper, seeded and chopped
1 medium purple onion, thinly sliced
¾ cup dried currants
1 Granny Smith or tart apple, cored and chopped
¼ cup capers
½ teaspoon peeled and grated fresh gingerroot
½ cup toasted slivered almonds

DRESSING:
½ cup white wine tarragon vinegar
1 tablespoon sugar
½ teaspoon salt
freshly ground black pepper
1 teaspoon dry mustard
½ teaspoon ground mace
½ teaspoon ground cardamom
¼ teaspoon ground cinnamon
¼ teaspoon cayenne pepper
2 teaspoons curry powder, or garam marsala *
¾ cup vegetable oil

*Available in gourmet or natural food stores

1. Mix the rice, pepper, onion, currants, apple, capers, gingerroot, and almonds together in a large bowl.

2. Place all of the ingredients except the oil for the dressing in a blender or food processor and process until blended. While the machine is running, slowly drizzle in the oil until the mixture is creamy. Pour the dressing over the salad and chill for several hours. Pack the salad in a 2-quart covered container to transport to the picnic. This salad can be served at room or "air" temperature.

CARROTS WITH MINTED MUSTARD VINAIGRETTE
▼▼▼▼▼▼▼▼▼▼▼▼▼

Serves 8   Preparation Time: 40 minutes

6 large carrots, peeled and sliced ⅛ inch thick
¼cup chopped fresh mint leaves

Mustard Vinaigrette:
¼ cup lemon vinegar or lemon juice
2 tablespoons olive oil
2 tablespoons vegetable oil
1 tablespoon Dijon mustard
¼ teaspoon salt
¼ teaspoon white pepper

1. Steam the carrots for 10 minutes or until crisp tender, or cook them in a microwave oven for 5 to 8 minutes until crisp tender. Mix the hot carrots in a bowl with the vinegar, oils, mustard, salt, and pepper. Cover the bowl and cool in the refrigerator for about 30 minutes.

2. Sprinkle the mint on the cooled carrots and pack in a covered container to take to the picnic. These carrots are best served at "air" temperature.

STRAWBERRY COOKIES

▼▼▼▼▼▼▼▼▼▼▼▼▼

To make these whimsical cookies, you will need a strawberry-shaped cookie cutter which is available in country stores or gourmet shops. Without the strawberry-shaped cutter, you will have a tender, lemon-flavored sugar cookie in the shape of your choice.

Makes 5 dozen   Preparation Time: 15 minutes   Chilling Time: 1 hour   Baking Time: 20 minutes

½ cup solid shortening
¾ cup sugar
¼ cup milk
1 egg, slightly beaten
1 teaspoon pure almond extract
2 teaspoons grated lemon rind
2½ cups unsifted all-purpose flour
2 teaspoons baking powder
red and green food coloring

1. In the large bowl of an electric mixer, cream the shortening and sugar at medium speed until light and fluffy. Beat in the milk, egg, almond extract, and lemon rind until well blended.

2. Sift together the flour and baking powder into a medium-size bowl and gradually add to the creamed mixture until the dough is well mixed.

3. Wrap the dough in plastic wrap and chill for 1 hour or until firm.

4. Preheat the oven to 350° F.

5. Divide the dough in half, form each half into a flattened ball, and place one on a lightly floured surface.

Roll the dough to ⅛ inch thickness. Using the strawberry cutter, cut out the cookies and place them on an ungreased baking sheet. With a skewer, make small indentations to resemble strawberry seeds on the cookies. Put 1 tablespoon of water in two small dishes and add a few drops of the food coloring. Brush the stems of the cookies lightly with the green food coloring and the fruit with the red food coloring.

6. Bake the cookies for 8 minutes or until lightly browned around the edges. Remove from the baking sheet and cool on wire racks. Repeat with the second ball of dough. To save time, you might make only a special few with the strawberry cutter and the remaining ones the shape of your choice.

SPORTS BOOSTER PICNIC

When people engage in monumental athletic feats such as marathons or triathlons, it is up to their friends to support their efforts. Having attempted to cheer on a marathoner, I know it is no small feat to follow the course and be supportive. All deserve a celebration at the end of such an event. Some friends who live on the New England seacoast typically celebrate with lobster rolls as the main course and plenty of liquid refreshment. This picnic is best held in a backyard or on a deck rather than at the end of the race, to give the athletes time to recover and shower.

MENU
BROCCOLI SOUP*

LOBSTER ROLLS*

HUGE TOSSED SALAD*

FRESH LEMONADE* OR COLD BEER OR CHAMPAGNE FRAMBOISE*

BROCCOLI SOUP
▼▼▼▼▼▼▼▼▼▼▼▼▼▼

Serves 8   Preparation Time: 30 minutes

1 large bunch broccoli
6 tablespoons butter
½ cup all-purpose flour
6 cups chicken stock
½ cup plain yogurt
½ cup heavy cream, light cream, or milk
¼ teaspoon salt
1 teaspoon dried tarragon
¼ teaspoon ground nutmeg
¼ teaspoon white pepper

1. Wash the broccoli and trim off 1 cup of the florets and reserve for a garnish. Cut the rest of the broccoli into small pieces, including the stems.

2. In a large steamer, steam the broccoli pieces for about 5 minutes or until crisp tender. Set aside. Also, steam the garnish florets.

3. Melt the butter in a large saucepan. Add the flour and cook over low heat for 1 minute while the mixture bubbles. Add the stock and cook, stirring with a whisk until the mixture begins to boil and thicken.

4. Add the broccoli pieces and simmer on low heat for 10 minutes.

5. In batches, process the soup in a blender until smooth. Return the soup to the saucepan and bring just to a boil. Add the yogurt, cream, salt, tarragon, nutmeg, and pepper. Pour the soup into heated thermos bottles and bring to the picnic. Store the garnish in a seal-lock plastic bag in the cooler.

6. Serve the soup in mugs and garnish with the reserved broccoli florets.

Note: This soup can be chilled for 2 hours and served cold.

LOBSTER ROLLS
▼▼▼▼▼▼▼▼▼▼▼▼▼

Serves 8   Preparation Time: 30 minutes

3 cups cooked lobster meat
½ cup chopped celery
4 green onions, chopped with some green tops
1 tablespoon melted butter
1 tablespoon lemon juice
8 deli rolls

HOMEMADE MAYONNAISE:
1 egg
2 egg yolks
¼ cup lemon juice
1 tablespoon Dijon mustard
¼ teaspoon salt
freshly ground black pepper
1 cup corn oil

1. Combine the lobster, celery, onions, melted butter, and the 1 tablespoon lemon juice in a medium-size bowl and stir to blend.

2. Make the mayonnaise by combining the egg, egg yolks, ¼ cup lemon juice, mustard, salt, and pepper in a food processor. Process until blended.

3. With the machine running, slowly drizzle the oil through the feed tube until the mayonnaise is thick.

4. Add the mayonnaise to the lobster mixture and stir to blend.

5. Put the lobster mixture in a covered container and store until time to go to the picnic. Make the lobster rolls at the picnic by slicing the rolls and spreading on the lobster mixture.

HUGE TOSSED SALAD
▼▼▼▼▼▼▼▼▼▼▼▼▼

The secret of a great tossed salad is having wonderful fresh greens that are clean, crisp, and dry. A lettuce spinner is most helpful.

Serves 8   Preparation Time: 30 minutes

1 large head red lettuce
1 large head green garden lettuce, or curly endive
An assortment of any or all of the following vegetables:
chunks of tomatoes, thinly sliced cucumbers,
thinly sliced purple onions, drained mandarin oranges, sliced mushrooms,
artichoke hearts, sliced avocado

Mustard Vinaigrette (see page 90), or your favorite salad dressing

1. Immerse the lettuce in a sink full of cold water. Place some of the leaves in a lettuce spinner and spin dry. Drain the excess water from the spinner and repeat the process until all the lettuce is washed and dried. Place the washed lettuce in a large plastic bag and store in the refrigerator until ready to go to the picnic.

2. Bring all the salad ingredients wrapped separately and construct the salad in a large bowl at the picnic. Toss it all together and enjoy.

FRESH LEMONADE
▼▼▼▼▼▼▼▼▼▼▼▼▼

Serves 8   Preparation Time: 15 minutes

1 cup sugar
5 cups cold water
2 teaspoons grated lemon rind
juice of 8 lemons
mint sprigs for garnish

1. Combine all the ingredients, except the mint in a large pitcher and chill.

2. Pour into cold thermos bottles to bring to the picnic, or just bring the cold pitcher. Serve in glasses and top each glass with a mint sprig.

CHAMPAGNE FRAMBOISE
▼▼▼▼▼▼▼▼▼▼▼▼▼

Serves 8   Preparation Time: 10 minutes

1 pint fresh raspberries
⅓ cup raspberry syrup or cassis
2 bottles champagne or sparkling wine, chilled

1. Soak the raspberries in the syrup or cassis for 5 minutes.

2. Place several tablespoons of the raspberry mixture in each glass. Fill with champagne and serve immediately.

STORE-BOUGHT PICNICS

Not all picnics are planned ahead. Nor is it always possible to prepare the food for a picnic. Enter the "Store-bought Picnic." Picnics are especially appealing when on vacation. It could mean a stop at the fast-food store and taking the bags to a park bench, or stopping at a delicatessen for favorite sandwiches, or going to a gourmet shop and selecting soups, salads, breads and cheeses, a luscious dessert, and fine wines. When in the city, find a great deli and a park.

While traveling through the French countryside one summer, my husband and I alternated between long, many course meals in special restaurants and simple picnics. On picnic days, we wandered through small, outdoor village markets for meats and cheeses. Next we visited the local *boulanger* for a fresh, crusty baguette. The final stop was for a bottle of inexpensive local wine. Everything, including my Swiss army knife and a reed mat, went into our French market basket and we were ready to seek a lovely spot by the roadside.

CALIFORNIA WINE COUNTRY PICNIC — OAKVILLE GROCERY

A favorite California outing is wandering up Highway 29 through the Napa Valley, with leisurely stops at vineyards to sample their treasures. We made such a trip one April, which is before there is much growth on the vines, or many visitors clogging the single highway through the valley. The weather was superb, the vintners were chatty, and the picnic from the *Oakville Grocery* was outstanding.

The *Oakville Grocery* is crammed with wonderful wines and delicacies. The take-out counter offers an array of aromatic breads and spicy salads which are perfect for the spur-of-the-moment picnic on a sunny day. Just as you are leaving with your little containers of soups and salads and wondering what you will eat off of, you spot the sets of picnic plates, cups, napkins, and flatware in little plastic bags, stowed by the door. The next delightful task is to find a vineyard that welcomes picnickers and enjoy yourselves.

The *Oakville Grocery,* located on Highway 29 in Oakville, California, kindly sent us recipes from their caterers so that you can make up your own wine country picnic.

MENU
YAM AND CHILI SOUP*

ORIENTAL VEGETABLE SALAD*

PASTA PRIMAVERA*

TOMATO BASIL BREAD**

RASPBERRY BROWNIES**

CALIFORNIA WINE

WINE SUGGESTIONS:

From Eric Murray of the *Oakville Grocery*, Joseph Phelps Vineyards Gewurtztraminer,

"The spicy, floral character of the wine is a perfect foil for the spices,

while the slight sweetness is cooling, similar to a chutney served with curry" or Saintsbury's Garnet,

"A light bodied engagingly fruity Pinot Noir perfectly suited to picnic fare."

EXTRA ITEMS TO BRING:

SWISS ARMY KNIFE

** *These items are from the Alexis Baking Company in Napa, California.*

YAM AND CHILI SOUP

▼▼▼▼▼▼▼▼▼▼▼▼▼

The unusual combination of flavors makes this tasty soup a vintage California dish and a wonderful surprise to the palate. The smooth velvety texture offsets the hot chili flavor.

Serves 8   Preparation Time: 45 minutes   Make crème fraîche 24 hours ahead*

½ cup butter
1 large onion, thinly sliced
4 garlic cloves, crushed
¼ teaspoon ground cumin
1 to 2 cayenne chilies, seeded
2 1½ pounds yams, peeled and sliced
6 cups chicken stock
salt to taste

GARNISHES:
½ cup green onions, cut on bias
¼ cup chopped fresh cilantro
1 cup crème fraîche* (plain yogurt may be substituted)

* Make crème fraîche by mixing 1 cup heavy cream
and 1 cup sour cream and let sit at room temperature for 24 hours.

1. Melt the butter in a large pot. Sauté the onion and garlic with the cumin and chilies until the onions are soft. Add the yams and cook over low heat until the onions are golden and the yams are slightly coated, about 10 to 15 minutes.

2. Add the chicken stock, bring to boil, and simmer for 15 minutes until the yams are soft when pierced with a fork. Salt to taste.

3. Puree the soup in a food processor and then pass through a sieve. Pack in a thermos bottle until picnic time.

4. Garnish each serving with the green onions, cilantro, and a swirl of crème fraîche.

ORIENTAL VEGETABLE SALAD
▼▼▼▼▼▼▼▼▼▼▼▼▼

Serves 8   Preparation Time: 45 minutes   Chilling Time: 1 hour

1 large bunch broccoli, cut into florets and diagonal stalks, lightly blanched
1 cup celery, cut on bias
1 cup carrots, cut in half, thinly sliced on bias
2 small red bell peppers, cut into julienne strips
½ pound fresh green beans, lightly blanched
1 cup drained pickled baby corn
4 ounces shiitake mushrooms, stems removed, quartered, and blanched
6 green onions, cut on bias
2 ounces fresh water chestnuts, blanched
1 cup chopped fresh cilantro

DRESSING:
3 garlic cloves, finely chopped
1- to 2-inch piece gingerroot, peeled and grated
2 tablespoons plum sauce
¼ cup soy sauce
¼ cup sesame oil
½ cup peanut oil
2 tablespoons rice wine vinegar
3 tablespoons black sesame seeds

1. Combine all the vegetables in a large bowl.

2. Whisk together the ingredients for the dressing in a small bowl.

3. Pour the dressing over the prepared vegetables and toss well. Cover and chill for 1 hour before packing for the picnic.

PASTA PRIMAVERA
▼▼▼▼▼▼▼▼▼▼▼▼▼

Serves 8 to 10   Preparation Time: 45 minutes   Chilling Time: 1 hour

1 pound tricolor rotelle pasta, cooked al dente *and drained*
1 small bunch broccoli, cut into bite-size pieces and lightly blanched
½ pound cauliflower, cut into bite-size pieces and lightly blanched
½ cup cherry tomatoes
¾ cup red bell peppers, cut into 2-inch julienne strips (yellow or
green pepper optional for additional color)
¾ cup zucchini, cut into quarters
lengthwise and sliced in ¼-inch slices

GARLIC CREAM SAUCE:
1 egg yolk, at room temperature
1 to 2 garlic cloves, crushed
1 tablespoon lemon juice
¼ teaspoon salt
½ cup olive oil
¼ cup heavy cream

1. Combine the pasta and vegetables in a large bowl.

2. To make the cream sauce, mix the egg yolk, garlic, lemon juice, and salt in a food processor. With the machine running, slowly add the oil until the mixture is thick. Blend in the heavy cream and pour over the pasta and vegetables. Chill for at least 1 hour.

TOMATO BASIL BREAD
▼▼▼▼▼▼▼▼▼▼▼▼▼

The aroma and flavor of this colorful bread are reminiscent of pizza.

Makes 1 loaf   *Preparation Time: 30 minutes*   *Rising Time: 1 hour 30 minutes*   *Baking Time: 35 to 40 minutes*

2 tablespoons olive oil
½ cup chopped onions
2 garlic cloves, minced
1 tablespoon active dry yeast
2 cups warm water
¾ cup tomato puree
4 cups unbleached all-purpose flour
2 teaspoons salt
½ teaspoon sugar
1 tablespoon dried basil

1. In a medium-size saucepan, heat the oil and sauté the onions for about 10 minutes until soft. Add the garlic at the end of the cooking time. Let cool.

2. In a large bowl, dissolve the yeast in the warm water. Add the tomato puree and mix.

3. In a medium-size bowl, combine the dry ingredients and add to the yeast mixture. Add the onions, garlic, and oil and mix well.

4. Turn the dough out on a floured surface and knead until the dough is smooth and elastic. Return the dough to the bowl and cover with a damp cloth. Let it rise until doubled in size, about 1 hour and 30 minutes.

5. Punch down the dough and shape into a round free-form loaf and place on a greased baking sheet. Let it rise slightly while the oven is preheating.

6. Preheat the oven to 400° F.

7. Bake for 35 to 40 minutes, or until it is lightly browned and sounds hollow when tapped. Remove the loaf from the baking sheet and cool completely on a wire rack.

8. Either slice the loaf in advance, or bring a cutting board and a bread knife to the picnic. To transport to the picnic, put the loaf in a plastic bag and place in a bread basket, lined with a colorful napkin.

RASPBERRY BROWNIES
▼▼▼▼▼▼▼▼▼▼▼▼▼

A dense rich chocolate with a hint of raspberries combine to make a chocolate lover's dream.

Makes 16 brownies   *Preparation Time: 1 hour*   *Freezing Time: 30 minutes*   *Baking Time: 40 to 45 minutes*

4 ounces unsweetened chocolate
8 ounces unsalted butter
1 teaspoon salt
1 teaspoon pure vanilla extract
2 cups sugar
4 eggs
1 cup unbleached all-purpose flour
2 cups walnut pieces
1 scant cup raspberry preserves

1. Melt the chocolate and butter in a large, heavy saucepan over low heat, stirring occasionally.

2. Remove the pan from the heat and add the salt, vanilla, and sugar and mix well. Add the eggs, one at a time, mixing after each one. Add the flour and beat until smooth. Stir in the walnut pieces.

3. Pour **half** the batter into a greased 9-inch-by-13-inch baking pan and make a smooth surface. Freeze the batter for 30 minutes.

4. Preheat the oven to 350° F.

5. When the batter is frozen, spread the preserves on the batter in a thin layer. Pour the remaining batter over the preserves and gently smooth it over to cover the preserves.

6. Bake for 40 to 45 minutes, or until a tester inserted in the center comes out clean.

7. Cool the pan on a wire rack for 10 minutes before cutting the brownies. Cool the brownies completely on the wire rack.

8. Place the brownies on a pretty plate, cover them with plastic wrap, and pack in the picnic basket.

FALL FOLIAGE IN NEW ENGLAND PICNIC— TRUFFLES & SUCH

New England is famed for its brilliant display of color during the brief period before the leaves fly and the land becomes barren. Warm or crisp cool autumn weekends cry out for picnics. For some, a great pleasure is to pack a sumptuous feast and cart it off to a college football game for a traditional tailgate party. *Truffles & Such,* in Pittsfield, Massachusetts, offers an interesting selection of picnic fare available on four hours notice. To have plenty of food for a crowd, chef Irene Maston provided us with this fine selection of recipes.

MENU

BAKED BRIE WITH FRESH FRUIT*

ROAST PORK LOIN WITH MUSTARD AND CONSERVES*

MEDITERRANEAN TORTE*

BROCCOLI SALAD WITH CAESAR DRESSING*

SOUR CREAM APPLE PIE*

NATURAL FRUIT SODAS OR HOT COFFEE OR RED WINE

WINE SUGGESTIONS:

A medium-bodied Petit Chateaux from the Bordeaux Region or a California Merlot or for the adventurous,

a slightly chilled Bourgueil or Chinon from the Loire Valley

EXTRA ITEMS TO BRING:

CARD TABLE

COLORFUL TABLECLOTH AND NAPKINS

BLANKETS TO SIT ON

BAKED BRIE WITH FRESH FRUIT
▼▼▼▼▼▼▼▼▼▼▼▼▼

Serves 8   Preparation Time: 30 minutes   Chilling Time: 30 minutes   Baking Time: 10 to 12 minutes

one 1 pound package phyllo dough
½ cup melted butter
1½ pounds brie, cut into wedges
grapes
strawberries
apple wedges

1. Unroll the phyllo sheets and keep them covered with plastic wrap to prevent them from drying out. Remove two sheets of phyllo and brush the top one with butter.

2. Place a wedge of the brie diagonally on the phyllo sheet, about two inches from one corner. Fold the phyllo over the cheese and continue to roll the brie up in the phyllo sheet. Fold the ends in when half of the phyllo is used up. Finish rolling until the whole sheet is used up and the brie is neatly packaged. Brush the outside with butter to prevent flaking. Repeat the process until all the

brie is used up. Chill the brie for 30 minutes. The recipe can be made to this point and covered tightly with plastic wrap and stored in the refrigerator for a day.

3. Preheat the oven to 400° F.

4. On a baking sheet, bake the phyllo for 10 to 12 minutes or until golden brown.

5. Line a small basket with paper towels and gently place the brie in the basket. Arrange the fruit around it and pack it in the car.

ROAST PORK LOIN WITH MUSTARD AND CONSERVES
▼▼▼▼▼▼▼▼▼▼▼▼▼

Serves 8   Preparation Time: 40 minutes   Cooking Time: Several hours

3 to 4 pounds boneless pork loin
3 garlic cloves, minced
½ to ¾ cup coarse mustard
freshly ground black pepper
several fresh rosemary sprigs

FRUIT CONSERVES:
1 pound plums, peaches, or nectarines, pitted and chopped
1 ½ cups sugar
¾ cup raisins
¼ cup water
1 tablespoon grated orange rind
¼ cup orange juice
¼ cup chopped walnuts

1. Preheat the oven to 375° F.

2. Place the loin on a rack in a shallow roasting pan. Spread the outside with the minced garlic and cover with a thick layer of the mustard. Sprinkle with the pepper and rosemary.

3. Bake for 30 to 35 minutes per pound or to 160° F. internal temperature. Remove the meat from the pan and chill. Slice the meat, arrange it on a plate with the conserves. Cover the plate with plastic wrap to bring it to the picnic. Store the meat in the refrigerator until picnic time.

4. To make the conserves, combine the fruit, sugar, raisins, water, and rind in a large, heavy saucepan. Bring the mixture to a boil and simmer for 20 minutes.

5. Add the orange juice and simmer for 10 minutes more. Add the walnuts and simmer an additional 5 minutes. Remove the conserve from the heat, cool slightly, and chill. Put the conserve in a dish with a tight-fitting cover to pack in the picnic basket.

MEDITERRANEAN TORTE
▼▼▼▼▼▼▼▼▼▼▼▼▼

Serves 8   Preparation Time: 45 minutes   Baking Time: 45 minutes

1½ pounds bread dough (frozen store-bought dough, your favorite bread dough recipe, or
use the recipe from Calzones, page55)
8 ounces genoa salami, arranged in two 4-ounce stacks
1 quart cleaned whole small mushrooms
1 cup drained and dried black olives
8 ounces provolone, arranged in two 4-ounce stacks
8 ounces thinly sliced ham arranged in two 4-ounce stacks
1½ pounds frozen chopped spinach, thawed and squeezed dry
one 13¾-ounce can pimientos, drained and dried
1½ cups drained and dried artichoke quarters
1 egg yolk mixed with 1 tablespoon water

1. Preheat the oven to 350° F.

2. Use one quarter of the dough to roll out a 10-inch circle for the top. Set this piece aside.

3.a. Roll out the rest of the dough so it fills a 10-inch springform pan, with one inch of dough hanging over the edge. Arrange the filling in the following order from bottom to top by spreading each ingredient in a layer on top of the preceding one:

4 ounces of the salami   4 ounces of the ham
the mushrooms   the spinach
the olives   the pimientos
4 ounces of the provolone   the remaining 4 ounces of salami

3.b. Then fold the excess dough in over the filling and continue with:

the remaining 4 ounces of ham, ½ inch from the edge
the artichoke hearts
the remaining 4 ounces of provolone

4. Brush the edge of the dough with the egg glaze and place the top piece of dough on the edge. Brush the top with the glaze, prick a few times with a fork, and let the dough rise briefly. Bake for 45 minutes or until golden brown. Let the torte cool in the pan. Remove the sides and serve at room temperature. Store in the refrigerator. Cut the torte into pieces before wrapping it for the picnic.

BROCCOLI SALAD WITH CAESAR DRESSING
▼▼▼▼▼▼▼▼▼▼▼▼▼

Serves 8   Preparation Time: 15 minutes

6 cups broccoli florets, with 2-inch stems
ice water
½ cup sliced black olives
1 medium red onion, thinly sliced
1 medium red bell pepper, seeded and thinly sliced

DRESSING:
2 teaspoons Dijon mustard
2 egg yolks
2 teaspoons minced garlic
1 teaspoon capers
freshly ground black pepper
¼ cup grated Parmesan cheese
2 parsley sprigs
3 anchovy fillets
1 cup olive oil
2 tablespoons lemon juice
¼ cup red wine vinegar

1. Blanch the broccoli in boiling water for 1 minute or until bright green. Plunge immediately into the ice water.   Drain, place in a bowl, and toss with the olives, onion, and pepper.

2. To make the dressing, blend the mustard, egg yolks, garlic, capers, pepper, cheese, parsley, and anchovies in a food processor. Slowly drizzle in the oil. Add the lemon juice and wine vinegar. Pour over the broccoli and chill. Take to the picnic in a tightly covered dish.

SOUR CREAM APPLE PIE
▼▼▼▼▼▼▼▼▼▼▼▼▼

A wonderful alternative to old-fashioned apple pie. It keeps better, too, if there is any left over.

Makes 1 pie   Preparation Time: 20 minutes   Baking Time: 1 hour 15 minutes

one 9-inch pie shell, unbaked
6 tart baking apples, peeled, cored, and sliced
1½ cups sour cream
1 egg, beaten
½ cup sugar
¼ cup all-purpose flour

TOPPING:
½ cup melted butter
⅓ cup granulated sugar
⅓ cup firmly packed brown sugar
½ cup all-purpose flour
1 teaspoon ground cinnamon
1 cup chopped walnuts

1. Preheat the oven to 450° F.

2. Place the apples in a large bowl with the sour cream, egg, sugar, and flour. Toss all together until the apples are coated with the mixture.

3. Pour the apple mixture into the pie shell and bake for 10 minutes. Turn the oven down to 350° F. and bake for 35 to 40 minutes.

4. Mix the topping ingredients together in a medium-size bowl. Sprinkle over the pie. Bake an additional 15 to 20 minutes until the topping looks crunchy. Cool the pie on a wire rack and bring it to the picnic in the pan.

SUMMER IN THE BERKSHIRES PICNIC — CROSBY'S

The Berkshire Hills abound with sheltered glades, flowering meadows, and summer performing arts festivals. Picnicking ranges from the most casual to the well orchestrated. To combine spontaneity with elegance, choose your store and menu carefully. *Crosby's* of Lenox, Massachusetts, supplied the recipes for these enticing dishes. Bobbi Crosby, a popular Berkshire caterer, offers picnics by special reservations made forty-eight hours in advance. In summer months, picnic menus are available for those who wish to make some advance planning for their vacation picnic in the Berkshires. Bobbie Crosby generously provided these recipes for those who are willing to do the cooking themselves.

MENU
SHREDDED CARROTS WITH WALNUT VINAIGRETTE*
SESAME CHICKEN WINGS*
TORTELLINI SALAD WITH PINENUTS*
SOUR CREAM CHOCOLATE CAKE*
ICED COFFEE OR TEA OR CHILLED WHITE WINE
WINE SUGGESTIONS:
A Vernaccia or a San Gimignano or on the lighter side, a Dry Galestro from Antinori or Ricasoli

EXTRA ITEMS TO BRING:
BLANKETS
BEACH CHAIRS
CANDLES FOR EVENING
BOUQUET OF WILD FLOWERS

SHREDDED CARROTS WITH WALNUT VINAIGRETTE
▼▼▼▼▼▼▼▼▼▼▼▼▼

Serves 8   Preparation Time: 30 minutes

4 medium carrots, peeled and finely grated
¼ cup finely chopped fresh parsley

WALNUT VINAIGRETTE:
2 tablespoons white wine tarragon vinegar
1 tablespoon Dijon mustard
¼ teaspoon sugar
¼ teaspoon salt
1 garlic clove, finely minced
2 tablespoons walnut oil
¼ cup peanut oil

1. Place the shredded carrots and parsley in a medium-size bowl.

2. To make the vinaigrette, combine the vinegar, mustard, sugar, salt, and garlic in a small bowl. Slowly whisk in the oils until the dressing is well blended. Pour the vinaigrette over the carrots and stir to combine. Place in a covered serving bowl and chill until ready to take to the picnic.

SESAME CHICKEN WINGS
▼▼▼▼▼▼▼▼▼▼▼▼▼

A truly tasty dish that is simple to prepare. The secret is a long period of marinating.

Serves 8   *Preparation Time: 10 minutes*   *Marinating Time: Overnight*   *Baking Time: 30 minutes*

16 chicken wings
¼ cup sesame seeds

Marinade:
1 cup soy sauce
¼ cup honey
¼ cup cider vinegar
1 tablespoon peeled and chopped fresh gingerroot
¼ cup sesame oil
1 garlic clove, minced
pinch cayenne pepper

1. Rinse the chicken wings in cold water and pat dry. Place them in a low-sided glass baking dish. Combine the marinating ingredients in a medium-size bowl and pour over the chicken.

2. Let the chicken marinate at least overnight, the longer the better.

3. Preheat the oven to 425° F.

4. Place the chicken in a roasting pan and brush with the marinade. Sprinkle the wings with the sesame seeds and bake for 30 minutes, or until they are browned and cooked through. Place the hot chicken on a serving plate and cool in the refrigerator. When cold, cover the chicken with plastic wrap and transport to the picnic.

TORTELLINI SALAD WITH PINENUTS
▼▼▼▼▼▼▼▼▼▼▼▼▼

Serves 8 generously   Preparation Time: 30 minutes

2 pounds fresh tortellini pasta
1 cup seeded and chopped green peppers
1 cup seeded and chopped red bell peppers
1 cup chopped green onions, with some green tops
½ cup chopped pinenuts
¼ cup chopped fresh basil
¼ cup chopped fresh dill
¼ cup grated Parmesan cheese

DRESSING:
¼ cup balsamic vinegar
1 garlic clove, minced
¼ teaspoon salt
freshly ground black pepper
¾ cup peanut oil

1. Cook the tortellini until it is *al dente* in a large pot of rapidly boiling water. The amount of time this takes will depend on the tortellini.

2. Drain the tortellini and place in a large bowl with the peppers, green onions, pinenuts, basil, dill, and cheese.

3. To make the dressing, combine the vinegar, garlic, salt, and pepper in a small bowl. Whisk in the oil until well combined. Pour the dressing over the tortellini and chill. Put the salad in a 2-quart covered bowl to bring to your picnic.

SOUR CREAM CHOCOLATE CAKE
▼▼▼▼▼▼▼▼▼▼▼▼▼

This moist cake is not only delicious, but easy to make.

Serves 8　　　*Preparation Time: 55 minutes*　　　*Baking Time: 50 to 55 minutes*

1 cup all-purpose flour
1 teaspoon baking powder
½ teaspoon baking soda
½ teaspoon salt
2 ounces unsweetened chocolate
1 ¼ cups sugar
1 tablespoon cocoa
⅓ cup boiling water
2 eggs
¾ cup softened unsalted butter
½ cup sour cream
1 teaspoon pure vanilla extract

ICING:
½ cup heavy cream
6 ounces semisweet or bittersweet chocolate, cut into medium-size pieces

1. Preheat the oven to 325° F.

2. In a large bowl, blend the flour, baking powder, baking soda, and salt. Set aside.

3. Place the chocolate, ¼ cup of the sugar and the cocoa in a food processor. Process the mixture until it resembles coarse crumbs. Add the boiling water and process until the chocolate melts, then add the eggs and process until combined. Add the butter, sour cream, and vanilla and process again. Finally, add the reserved dry ingredients and process until well blended.

4. Pour the batter into a greased and floured 8-inch springform pan. Bake for 50 to 55 minutes, or until the cake comes away from the sides of the pan.

5. Cool in the pan for about 10 minutes before removing the sides and bottom of the pan. Cool the cake on a wire rack. When completely cool, ice the cake on the rack so the excess icing can run off.

6. To make the icing, scald the cream in a heavy saucepan over medium heat. Add the chocolate and stir the mixture over the heat for 1 minute. Remove the icing from the heat and continue to stir until the chocolate is completely melted. When the icing is warm, not hot, spread it on the cake. Place the iced cake on a plate and store in a cool place so the icing can set before packing it for the picnic.

SANDY PICNICS

▼▼

Fresh air, open space, and the sound and smell of the sea make a picnic on the beach one of the most perfect picnics. Put children, sand, and water together and you have the ideal playground. Put food, young people of all ages, and a stretch of beach with crashing surf or gentle rollers together and you have the beginning of a perfect picnic. Add sunshine, a shady spot, some dune grass, blankets, and beach toys and be prepared for a great day. Whether on wide, wild stretches of the Pacific Coast, a more civilized East Coast beach, or a rocky shore, a sense of peace and relaxation comes from being close to the sea.

Whenever we are in California, we pack some food in a basket, head over the coastal range, and drive along Highway 1 until we find a section of deserted beach that appeals to our mood. Access to Atlantic beaches is not quite so carefree, but certainly possible with a little planning.

A special note: Bring a garbage bag and clean up everything. Remember, also, that what people throw overboard on boats ends up on somebody's beach. A trashy beach takes the romance away from the perfect picnic.

SPRING BREAKFAST ON THE BEACH PICNIC

For those who love the ocean and are lucky enough to live near it, a warm spring weekend is a call to the sea. Begin a glorious day with breakfast or brunch on the beach. A lakeside beach wouldn't be a bad way to celebrate the beginning of spring either.

MENU
HOT COFFEE WITH CINNAMON WHIPPED CREAM
CURRANT OAT SCONES* AND FRUIT PRESERVES
CHEESE CASSEROLE*
CHILLED ASPARAGUS*
FRESH ORANGE JUICE OR SANGRIA*

EXTRA ITEMS TO BRING:
A COOLER
BEACH BLANKETS OR TOWELS
BEACH CHAIRS

CURRANT OAT SCONES
▼▼▼▼▼▼▼▼▼▼▼▼▼

Makes 12 scones   Preparation Time: 30 minutes

1½ cups all-purpose flour
¾ cup old-fashioned rolled oats
1 tablespoon baking powder
¼ cup sugar
¼ teaspoon salt
¼ cup very cold butter, cut into chunks
2 eggs, well beaten
¼ cup heavy cream
½ cup currants
sweet butter and fruit preserves to serve with the scones

1. Preheat the oven to 400° F.

2. Place the flour, oats, baking powder, sugar, and salt in a food processor. Process briefly. With the motor running, add the butter and process until the mixture resembles coarse crumbs.

3. Mix the eggs and cream together in a small bowl and with the motor running, add to the flour mixture. Process until the dough forms a ball.

4. On a lightly floured surface, knead the currants into the dough until they are evenly distributed. Pat the dough into a circle that is approximately 7 to 8 inches in diameter and 1 inch thick.

5. Cut the circle in half and cut each half into six wedge-shaped pieces. Place the scones on an ungreased baking sheet. Bake for 15 minutes or until golden brown. Wrap them in a fresh cloth napkin, place in a small basket, and hope that they are still warm by the time you get to the beach. Serve with the sweet butter and fruit preserves.

CHEESE CASSEROLE
▼▼▼▼▼▼▼▼▼▼▼▼▼

Serves 8   Preparation Time: 30 minutes   Standing Time: Overnight, plus 30 minutes
Baking Time: 50 to 60 minutes

9 slices whole-wheat bread, cut into thirds
1 medium onion, chopped
1 pound cheddar cheese, grated
4 eggs, slightly beaten
3 cups milk
1 teaspoon dry mustard
1 tablespoon Worcestershire sauce
½ teaspoon salt
¼ teaspoon white pepper
dash cayenne pepper

1. In a greased 2-quart casserole dish, place nine pieces of the bread. Sprinkle with ⅓ of the onions and ⅓ of the cheese. Repeat this layering until all of these ingredients are used.

2. In a 1-quart measuring cup, whisk together the eggs, milk, mustard, Worcestershire sauce, salt, pepper, and cayenne. Pour over the bread, onions, and cheese. Cover the casserole with plastic wrap and store in the refrigerator overnight.

3. Remove the casserole from the refrigerator 30 minutes before baking.

4. Preheat the oven to 325° F.

5. Bake the casserole for 50 to 60 minutes. The casserole will be puffy as it comes out of the oven. It will deflate slightly as it cools, but the flavor will remain the same. Wrap the casserole in a towel to keep it warm when you take it to the beach.

CHILLED ASPARAGUS
▼▼▼▼▼▼▼▼▼▼▼▼▼

Serves 8   Preparation Time: 15 minutes   Chilling Time: 1 hour

2 pounds fresh spring asparagus, washed and trimmed
¼ cup Lemon Butter *(see page 131)*

1. Steam the asparagus for about 15 minutes until crisp tender.

2. Spread the asparagus stems out in a low, flat dish and cover the tips with lemon butter.

3. Cover the bowl and chill for 1 hour.

SANGRIA
▼▼▼▼▼▼▼▼▼▼▼▼▼

My brother, who lived in Spain for three years, devised this recipe and considers it most like what he found in Madrid.

Serves 8 to 12   Preparation Time: 15 minutes

2 ounces brandy
2 cups Triple Sec
one 1 liter Tom Collins mix
1 to 1.5 liters red wine
1 orange, thinly sliced
2 apples, cored and thinly sliced
lots of ice

1. Combine all the ingredients except the ice.

2. Fill two large pitchers with ice and pour the sangria over the ice. Wrap the pitchers in blankets and transport to the beach.

SUMMER BEACH PICNIC

This is the classic picnic of the summer. Imagine a clear, hot, dry day with an intense blue sky reflecting off the water and white sand. The endless crashing of waves on the beach is the musical background for your day in the sun. For a hot day at the beach, you want to bring plenty of cold drinks. In addition to the menu suggestions, a jug of ice water would be a welcome addition. It is unlikely that you will find much shade on the beach, so cover the food chest with several layers of blankets to make it as shady as possible. Choose a beach where cooking is permitted.

MENU
PHYLLO TURNOVERS*
GRILLED TUNA WITH LIME*
GARDEN FRESH TOMATOES WITH BASIL AND BALSAMIC VINEGAR*
MARINATED PASTA SALAD*
FRESH PEACH ICE CREAM* AND OMI'S COCOA CAKE*
COLD IMPORTED BEER OR SPARKLING WATER OR CHILLED WHITE WINE
WINE SUGGESTIONS:
A fine jug wine in 1.5 liter bottle of Robert Mondavi White Table or Torres Vina Sol or Fetzer Premium White

EXTRA ITEMS TO BRING:
CUTTING BOARD
SHARP KNIFE
PICNIC PLATTER FOR TUNA
SUN SCREEN
PLENTY OF BEACH TOWELS
PADDLE BALL
CHARCOAL AND STARTER
HIBACHI
MATCHES
BEACH UMBRELLAS

PHYLLO TURNOVERS
▼▼▼▼▼▼▼▼▼▼▼▼▼

Serves 8   Preparation Time: 30 minutes   Baking Time: 15 minutes

1 tablespoon olive oil
1 medium onion, chopped
3 cups finely chopped broccoli
1 egg
1 slice dry Swedish rye bread, crumbed
1 cup grated cheddar cheese
1 tablespoon lemon juice
½ teaspoon salt
¼ teaspoon white pepper
½ package phyllo dough
½ cup melted butter
2 tablespoons fennel seed

1. In a medium-size skillet, heat the oil and sauté the onion until soft. Place the onions in a large bowl.

2. Steam the broccoli for 5 to 10 minutes until tender, but still bright green. Add the broccoli to the onions. Mix in the egg, bread crumbs, cheese, lemon juice, salt, and pepper and set aside the broccoli mixture.

3. Preheat the oven to 375° F.

4. Before opening the phyllo dough, clear a work surface that is approximately 2½-feet-by-2-feet. Have a clean, damp dish towel available for covering the phyllo. Place the butter within reach as well as a baking sheet. Open the phyllo and lay one sheet on the work surface with the long side facing you. Lightly brush the sheet with some melted butter, place another sheet of phyllo on top of the first and brush it with butter. Repeat this process one more, so you have three layers of phyllo. Cover the remaining phyllo with the damp cloth so it won't dry out.

5. With scissors, cut the layered dough crosswise into six equal strips. One inch from the end of each strip near you, place a heaping tablespoon of the filling. Fold a triangle of the dough over the filling and continue to fold the dough as if you were folding a flag. Place the triangle on the baking sheet, lightly brush with butter and sprinkle with a few fennel seeds. Repeat this procedure until you have about thirty triangles. Bake for 15 minutes or until golden brown. Cool the triangles on wire racks and pack them gently in a covered tin to transport to the picnic. These can be made ahead and frozen either before or after baking.

GRILLED TUNA WITH LIME
▼▼▼▼▼▼▼▼▼▼▼▼▼

Serves 8   Preparation Time: 20 minutes

2½ to 3 pounds tuna steaks
1 cup marinade used for Chicken Fillets *(see page 32)*
2 limes, cut into wedges

1. Rinse the tuna and pat dry. Place in a low-sided container with a tight-fitting cover. Pour the marinade over the tuna, cover the dish, and pack in the cooler. Place the lime wedges in a plastic bag.

2. When you get to the beach, start a charcoal fire in the hibachi. When the coals are hot, grill the tuna 5 to 7 minutes on each side, brushing frequently with the marinade. Place the tuna on a picnic platter and surround with the lime wedges.

GARDEN FRESH TOMATOES WITH BASIL AND BALSAMIC VINEGAR
▼▼▼▼▼▼▼▼▼▼▼▼▼

This simple dish is totally dependent on fresh garden tomatoes and fresh basil and the rich taste of balsamic vinegar. Genetically engineered tomatoes that last in the supermarket for a week cannot be substituted. It is a treat of summer for tomato lovers.

Serves 8   Preparation Time: 10 minutes

4 large fresh garden tomatoes
8 fresh basil leaves
½ cup balsamic vinegar

1. Before going on the picnic, wash the tomatoes, remove the tops, and place the tomatoes in a low-covered dish with the basil leaves. Measure out the vinegar and place it in a small jar with a tight-fitting lid. Bring a small cutting board, and your tomato cutting knife.

2. At the picnic, just before serving, slice the tomatoes into ¼-to½-inch slices and arrange on the low dish. Chop the basil. Drizzle the vinegar over the tomatoes and sprinkle with the basil. So simple and so good.

Note: Casks of balsamic vinegar are family heirlooms in northern Italy. Bottles are available to us in gourmet shops and natural food stores.

MARINATED PASTA SALAD
▼▼▼▼▼▼▼▼▼▼▼▼▼

Serves 8   Preparation Time: 45 minutes   Chilling Time: 1 hour

¾ pound tricolor rotelle pasta
⅓ cup olive oil
⅓ cup red wine vinegar
½ teaspoon salt
4 to 5 fresh basil leaves
1 medium green pepper, seeded and chopped
¼ cup seeded and chopped red bell pepper
1 small purple onion, chopped
½ cup minced fresh parsley
¼ cup sliced black olives
¼ cup marinated artichoke hearts
freshly ground black pepper

1. In a large pot of boiling salted water, over high heat, cook the pasta for 15 minutes or until *al dente*. Drain the pasta through a colander and rinse quickly with cold water.

2. Place the pasta in a large bowl and toss with the oil, vinegar, and salt. Chill the pasta for 1 hour.

3. Meanwhile, prepare the basil, peppers, onion, parsley, olives, and artichoke hearts. When the pasta is cold, add those ingredients and toss well. Grind pepper over all and mix again. Store the salad in a 2 quart covered container in the refrigerator until packing time.

FRESH PEACH ICE CREAM
▼▼▼▼▼▼▼▼▼▼▼▼▼

Modern technology allows us to take fresh homemade ice cream to the beach with ease. The secret is having a Donvier-type ice cream maker with a metal container filled with a supercoolant. You place the container in the freezer overnight and it becomes so cold that the ice cream mixture freezes on contact. The metal container fits into a large cup with a churn. This entire apparatus can be stored in the freezer until packing time and then placed in the cooler for transporting to the beach.

Serves 8   Preparation Time: 20 minutes

2 cups half-and-half
1 cup milk
3 fresh peaches, peeled, chopped, and mashed
¼ teaspoon pure vanilla extract
¾ cup sugar
a chill frost ice-cream maker

1. Place all the ingredients in a large bowl and mix well.

2. Pour the mixture into the supercold metal container and follow the manufacturer's directions for churning. Store the ice cream in the freezer until packing time.

Wrap the entire ice cream maker in a tablecloth and put it into the picnic cooler. Ours sat in 90° F. heat for three hours one day and the ice cream was still frozen when we ate it.

OMI'S COCOA CAKE
▼▼▼▼▼▼▼▼▼▼▼▼▼

My grandmother enjoyed good food and did not particularly like to cook. Here is her easily prepared version of a German tort which was relished at many a "kaffee klatch."

Makes 1 cake   Preparation Time: 45 minutes   Baking Time: 15 to 20 minutes

Cake:
2 tablespoons softened butter
1 cup sugar
½ cup cold water
2 tablespoons cocoa
1 teaspoon pure vanilla extract
2 eggs, well beaten
1 cup all-purpose flour
1 teaspoon baking powder

Filling:
1 cup milk
¾ cup sugar
¼ cup cocoa
2 tablespoons softened butter
1 cup heavy cream, whipped

1. Preheat the oven to 350° F.

2. In a large bowl, cream the butter and sugar until thoroughly blended. With a whisk, beat in the water, cocoa, vanilla, and eggs until the mixture is well mixed.

3. Sift the flour and baking powder together into a small bowl and stir into the cocoa mixture. Pour the batter into two greased and floured 9-inch round cake pans and

bake for 15 to 20 minutes, or until a tester inserted in the center comes out clean. Cool the cakes on wire racks in the pans for 10 minutes. Remove from the pans and continue cooling on wire racks.

4. While the cake is baking, make the filling. Place the milk, sugar, cocoa, and butter in a large saucepan and cook over medium heat for 10 to 15 minutes, or until the mixture thickens. Stir occasionally in the beginning and constantly at the end. Remove from the heat and continue stirring while the mixture is cooling. The filling will resemble a fudge sauce.

5. Place one of the layers on a plate and cover the top with the filling. Carefully place the second layer on top of the filling. Cover the top layer with the whipped cream. Put the cake in a covered box for transporting to the picnic. Store in the refrigerator until travel time.

AUTUMN BEACH PICNIC

The image of gathering around a roaring beach fire with a kettle of steaming clams and lobsters carefully balanced on the coals is picturesque and inviting. The beach fire, however, may not be allowed and the cooking results may be problematic. Instead, order the lobsters and clams already cooked from the local seaside fish market. Put them in an old cooler to keep hot while carting them to a secluded spot on the beach.

One such memorable picnic was the day after Thanksgiving on the New Hampshire coast. You may wonder that anyone would want to eat anything other than turkey sandwiches, but we forced ourselves to enjoy this seafood feast. Parkas and a brisk fire helped to keep the cold wind away.

MENU
STEAMED CLAMS
CORN PUDDING*
RED LETTUCE SALAD*
BOILED LOBSTERS WITH LEMON BUTTER*
ORANGE MOUSSE*
HOT COFFEE OR RED WINE
WINE SUGGESTIONS:
A Beaujolais-Villages from Duboeuf or Louis Jadot

EXTRA ITEMS TO BRING:
PARKAS, HATS, AND GLOVES (NOT A PICNIC FOR THE FAINTHEARTED)
AN OLD COOLER FOR THE HOT SEAFOOD

CORN PUDDING
▼▼▼▼▼▼▼▼▼▼▼▼▼

Serves 8   Preparation Time: 10 minutes   Baking Time: 1 hour 15 minutes

two 10-ounce packages frozen corn, thawed and drained
3 eggs, well beaten
¼ cup all-purpose flour
1 tablespoon sugar
½ teaspoon salt
¼ teaspoon freshly ground black pepper
dash ground nutmeg
2 tablespoons melted butter
2 cups milk or light cream

1. Preheat oven to 325° F.

2. In a medium-size bowl, combine the corn and eggs.

3. Add the flour, sugar, salt, pepper, and nutmeg and mix well. Add the butter and milk or cream and mix again.

4. Pour the pudding mixture into a greased 1½-quart casserole dish and bake uncovered for 1 hour and 15 minutes or until set.

5. Cool slightly and store in the refrigerator. Cover the cold pudding carefully for transporting to the beach and serve it at "air" temperature.

RED LETTUCE SALAD
▼▼▼▼▼▼▼▼▼▼▼▼▼

Serves 8   Preparation Time: 15 minutes

1 large head red lettuce, washed, dried, crisped, and torn into small pieces
1 medium purple onion, thinly sliced
1 cup drained mandarin oranges
1 ripe avocado, peeled and sliced

Light Vinaigrette:
3 tablespoons white wine tarragon vinegar
1 tablespoon lemon juice
1 teaspoon dry mustard
1 teaspoon sugar
¼ teaspoon salt
freshly ground black pepper
¾ cup vegetable oil

1. Place the lettuce, onion, oranges, and avocado in a large traveling salad bowl. Cover with plastic wrap and store in the refrigerator until travel time. Wrap the bowl in a tablecloth and pack in the picnic basket.

2. Place the vinegar, lemon juice, mustard, sugar, salt, and pepper in a blender and mix well. Slowly drizzle in the oil and blend until creamy. Store in a container with a tight-fitting lid and pack in the picnic basket. Toss the salad with the dressing at the picnic.

LEMON BUTTER
▼▼▼▼▼▼▼▼▼▼▼▼▼

Makes ¾ cup   Preparation Time: 5 minutes

½ cup melted butter
¼ cup lemon juice
¼ teaspoon freshly ground black pepper

1. Blend the butter, lemon juice, and pepper and serve warm with the lobsters.

ORANGE MOUSSE
▼▼▼▼▼▼▼▼▼▼▼▼▼

Serves 8   Preparation Time: 30 minutes   Chilling Time: 1 to 2 hours

1 package unflavored gelatin
¼ cup lemon juice
3 eggs, separated; reserve at room temperature
½ cup sugar
2 tablespoons grated orange rind
juice of 2 oranges
¼ teaspoon salt
1 teaspoon pure vanilla extract
2 tablespoons Cointreau liqueur
1 cup heavy cream
2 tablespoons slivered toasted almonds (optional)

1. In a small bowl, sprinkle the gelatin over the lemon juice and let it sit for 5 minutes until the gelatin softens.

2. In a large saucepan, whisk together the egg yolks and ¼ cup of the sugar. Whisk in the orange rind, orange juice, and salt and cook over medium heat, stirring constantly for about 3 minutes until the mixture thickens slightly.

3. Remove the orange mixture from the heat and stir in the softened gelatin. Add the vanilla and Cointreau and stir well. Pour this mixture into a cold bowl and chill for 30 minutes to 1 hour until it begins to set and becomes thicker.

4. In the large bowl of an electric mixer, beat the egg whites at high speed until they are frothy. Continue beating while gradually adding the remaining ¼ cup sugar. Beat until stiff peaks form. Gently fold the egg whites into the thickened orange mixture.

5. Beat the heavy cream in the same electric mixer bowl until soft peaks form. Fold the whipped cream into the mousse. Spoon the mousse into 10-ounce clear plastic cups, sprinkle with the almonds if you wish, cover each cup with plastic wrap, and chill for at least 1 hour. Pack the cups in the cooler when ready to leave.

Note: An alternative is to freeze the individual mousse cups and serve frozen mousse, or let the cups thaw at the picnic.

ELEGANT PICNICS

Elegant picnics need not require formal attire. However, special care goes into the presentation of the food and the decor. Here is the opportunity to use the silver candlesticks, the linen tablecloth and napkins, and the crystal. Transporting these more fragile items requires care in packing and serving while outdoors. Plan to pack the china and crystal in many layers of extra napkins. Arrange them in a picnic basket with the most fragile items on top. For an elegant picnic, be extravagant in the show you put on. Always have flowers, and in the evening, candlelight is a must. For the food, looking good is almost as important as tasting good.

MUSICAL FESTIVAL PICNIC

Summer music festivals abound — Tanglewood in the Berkshires, Ravinia in Chicago, Wolf Trap in Washington — in all parts of the country. Competition can be fierce for elegant picnics on the grassy lawns of these outdoor concert halls. What can be more elegant than dining in style to live symphony music on a star-filled evening.

MENU
COLD ZUCCHINI SOUP*

CHINESE CHICKEN SALAD WITH FRIED WON TONS*

FRESH PEACHES AND PECAN BARS*

SUN TEA OR CHILLED WHITE WINE

WINE SUGGESTIONS:

A Verdicchio San Cigmano from Italy or a lush California or

Australian Chardonnay

EXTRA ITEMS TO BRING:

CANDLES AND CANDLESTICKS, SILVER PREFERRED

HURRICANE LAMPS ARE HELPFUL, IF THERE IS A BREEZE

LINEN NAPKINS AND TABLECLOTH

CHINA AND GLASSWARE

BOUQUET OF FLOWERS

COLD ZUCCHINI SOUP
▼▼▼▼▼▼▼▼▼▼▼▼▼

Serves 8   Preparation Time: 30 minutes   Chilling Time: 1 hour

3 medium zucchini, cut into 2-inch chunks
1 medium onion, chopped
1 thyme sprig, or 1 teaspoon dried thyme
1 parsley sprig
1 bay leaf
4½ cups chicken stock (homemade, if possible)
1 tablespoon lemon juice
½ teaspoon salt
¼ teaspoon white pepper
1½ cups plain yogurt

1. Place the zucchini, onion, thyme, parsley, and bay leaf in a medium-size saucepan with 1 cup of the chicken stock and bring to a boil over high heat. Simmer the mixture for about 10 minutes, or until the zucchini is tender. Remove the thyme sprig, parsley sprig, and bay leaf and puree the mixture in a blender or food processor until it is of uniform consistency.

2. For a smooth soup, strain the puree by pressing it through a strainer or sieve with the back of a spoon. An unstrained soup will have a slight texture to it. Add the remaining chicken stock, lemon juice, salt, pepper, and yogurt and stir well to blend. Pour the soup into a 1½-quart covered container and chill for at least 1 hour before packing in the cooler.

CHINESE CHICKEN SALAD WITH FRIED WON TONS
▼▼▼▼▼▼▼▼▼▼▼▼▼

Larrie brought this salad as her contribution to one of our Tanglewood Picnics. We loved it. Over the years it has evolved somewhat, but the essence has remained the same. This salad became the mainstay of my picnic business. It's fun to take on a picnic because it has so many parts.

Serves 8   Preparation Time for salad: 45 minutes   Cooking Time for won tons: 30 minutes

2 tablespoons sesame oil
1 garlic clove
4 slices fresh gingerroot, peeled and minced
8 chicken breast halves (slightly frozen to ease cutting),
skinned, boned, and cut into ¼-inch-by-2-inch strips
¼ cup sesame seeds
4 green onions, cut into 1-inch julienne with some green tops
¼ cup slivered almonds
½ head red leaf lettuce, washed, dried, and shredded

DRESSING:
*2 teaspoons mirin (sweet cooking sake) **
2 tablespoons rice vinegar
1 garlic clove, minced
1 teaspoon peeled and grated gingerroot
2 tablespoons soy sauce
1 tablespoon lemon juice
1 tablespoon dry mustard
½ teaspoon salt
freshly ground black pepper
¼ cup sesame oil
½ cup corn oil

Fried Won Tons:
½ cup sesame oil (not the hot variety)
½ package won ton skins, cut into ¼-inch strips

* Available in natural food stores

1. Heat the 2 tablespoons of sesame oil over medium heat in a wok. Quickly brown the garlic and ginger and remove them from the wok. Discard. Add the strips of chicken in several batches and stir-fry the chicken for 2 minutes per batch, or until the chicken pieces are just cooked through. Remove the cooked chicken from the wok and place in a large bowl.

2. Add the sesame seeds, green onions, and almonds to the chicken and toss to mix well. Place the shredded lettuce in a seal-lock plastic bag and store in the refrigerator until packing time. Pack it in the top part of the cooler.

3. To make the dressing, place the mirin, vinegar, garlic, gingerroot, soy sauce, lemon juice, mustard, salt, and pepper in a blender or food processor and process until well blended. Slowly drizzle in the sesame and corn oils with the motor running until the dressing is creamy. Pour the dressing over the chicken and toss. Place the salad in a large covered bowl and chill in the refrigerator until time to pack in the cooler.

4. To fry the won tons, wipe out the wok with a paper towel and heat the ½ cup of sesame oil over medium-high heat in the wok. Test the oil temperature by adding one piece of won ton to it. If it burns immediately, the oil is too hot. If the won ton skin quickly turns a golden brown and puffs up slightly, the temperature is perfect. Add three or four pieces of won ton at a time and brown them. Remove the crispy brown won tons skins from the wok and drain on paper towels. When all the won tons are cooked, place them in a plastic bag and pack them on the top of the picnic basket.

5. When it is time to serve the salad, place a bed of shredded lettuce in the center of each plate and spoon a generous portion of chicken on top of the lettuce. Crumble a handful of the crispy won tons on top of the salad and enjoy a taste and texture treat. The remaining won tons can be munched on throughout the meal.

PECAN BARS

▼▼▼▼▼▼▼▼▼▼▼▼▼

Serves 8   Preparation Time: 20 minutes   Baking Time: 30 minutes

¾ cup softened butter
½ cup sugar
1 egg
1 teaspoon pure vanilla extract
1 teaspoon grated lemon rind
2 cups all-purpose flour
¼ teaspoon salt

TOPPING:
2¼ cups finely chopped pecans
¾ cup sugar
1 teaspoon ground cinnamon
4 egg whites, slightly beaten, at room temperature

1. Preheat the oven to 350° F.

2. In a large bowl, cream the butter and sugar until light and fluffy. Add the egg, vanilla, and lemon rind and mix well.

3. Sift the flour and salt into a medium-size bowl and add the mixture to the creamed ingredients in small amounts. Mix until well combined. Spread the dough evenly in a 15-inch-by-10-inch-by-1-inch pan and bake for 15 minutes or until lightly browned around the edges.

4. To make the topping, combine the pecans, sugar, cinnamon, and egg whites in a large, heavy saucepan and cook over low heat, stirring constantly for 2 minutes, or until the sugar is dissolved. Increase the heat to medium-high and continue to cook and stir for 2 to 3 minutes, or until the mixtures thickens, browns slightly, and comes away from the sides of the pan.

5. Spread the topping evenly over the top of the dough and bake for 15 minutes more. Cool the cookies in the pan for 5 minutes and then cut into ¾-inch-by-2-inch bars.

SUN TEA

▼▼▼▼▼▼▼▼▼▼▼▼▼

Makes 3 quarts   *Preparation Time: 1 morning*

6 tea bags, or 6 tablespoons loose tea
3 quarts cold water
¼ cup sugar or honey (optional)
2 mint sprigs (optional)
1 lemon, thinly sliced (optional)

1. Place the tea in a 1-gallon glass jar and add the cold water. Set the jar in a sunny window or outside in the sunshine for several hours until the tea has infused the water.

2. Strain the tea, add your choice of optional ingredients, and chill. Remove the lemon and mint and pour the tea into chilled thermos bottles and take to your picnic.

AFTER THE WEDDING BRUNCH PICNIC

When guests come from out of town to a wedding, a brunch the next day gives everyone a chance to unwind and visit in a relaxed way.

MENU
ZUCCHINI AND SAUSAGE PIE*

SMALL ASSORTED BAGELS*

SLICED SMOKED SALMON AND CREAM CHEESE WITH CAPERS

FRESH FRUIT BOWL KALEIDOSCOPE*

TANTE'S COFFEE CAKE*

SELECTED COFFEES

CHAMPAGNE MIMOSAS* OR FRUIT PUNCH*

WINE SUGGESTIONS:

An inexpensive Spanish Sparkling Wine or a good California Champagne such as Korbel Brut or Extra Dry

EXTRA ITEMS TO BRING:

BOUQUETS FROM THE RECEPTION

ZUCCHINI AND SAUSAGE PIE
▼▼▼▼▼▼▼▼▼▼▼▼▼

Serves 8   Preparation Time: 35 minutes   Baking Time: 40 minutes

¼ cup vegetable oil
2 cups shredded zucchini
1 medium onion, chopped
½ pound bulk sausage
2 cups grated Swiss cheese
1 cup milk
½ cup half-and-half
2 tablespoons grated Parmesan cheese
2 eggs, slightly beaten
1 cup all-purpose flour
½ teaspoon salt
¼ teaspoon white pepper
1 tablespoon melted butter
dash ground nutmeg

1. Preheat the oven to 400° F.

2. Heat the oil in a large skillet over medium heat and sauté the zucchini and onion for 5 minutes or until soft. Remove from the pan and put into a large bowl. Add the sausage to the skillet. Break up the sausage with a wooden spoon and cook over medium heat until the pink color is gone. Drain the sausage on paper towels.

3. Add the sausage to the zucchini and onion and mix. Then add the remaining ingredients. Mix well and pour into a 9-inch-by-9-inch square baking pan. Bake for 40 minutes, or until a knife inserted in the center comes out clean. Cool the pie in the pan on a wire rack. Cut into squares and serve to the guests.

FRESH FRUIT BOWL KALEIDOSCOPE
▼▼▼▼▼▼▼▼▼▼▼▼▼

Serves 8   Preparation Time: 30 minutes

2 nectarines, pitted and cut into 1-inch chunks
3 peaches, pitted and cut into 1-inch chunks
1 pint blueberries
2 Granny Smith apples, washed, cored, and cut into ½-inch cubes
1 small cantaloupe, seeded and cut into ½-inch cubes
2 pounds watermelon, seeded and cut into ½-inch cubes
1 cup green or red seedless grapes
2 tablespoons sugar
¼ cup Grand Marnier liqueur
1 cup raspberries

DRESSING:
1 cup plain yogurt
2 tablespoons lemon juice
2 tablespoons sugar

1. In a large bowl, mix the nectarines, peaches, blueberries, apples, cantaloupe, watermelon, grapes, and sugar. Pour the Grand Marnier over all and stir gently. Put the fruit in a glass serving bowl and sprinkle the raspberries over the top. Serve the fruit at room temperature.

2. To make the dressing, combine the yogurt, lemon juice, and sugar in a small bowl. Serve in a pretty dish alongside the fruit bowl.

TANTE'S COFFEE CAKE
▼▼▼▼▼▼▼▼▼▼▼▼▼

Makes 2 cakes   *Preparation Time: 25 minutes*   *Baking Time: 20 minutes*

¼ cup softened butter
¾ cup sugar
3 eggs
3 cups all-purpose flour
1 tablespoon baking powder
1 cup milk
1 teaspoon grated lemon rind
¼ to ½ cup melted butter
¼ cup sugar mixed with 1½ teaspoons ground cinnamon
½ cup sliced unblanched almonds

1. Preheat the oven to 350° F.

2. In the large bowl of an electric mixer, cream the softened butter and sugar until light and fluffy. Add the eggs and beat at medium speed until well blended.

3. Sift the flour and baking powder together in a medium-size bowl. At low speed, alternately add the flour mixture and milk to the creamed mixture and continue beating until thick and light colored. Stir in the lemon rind until well mixed.

4. Spread the batter evenly into two greased 9-inch-by-13-inch-by-1-inch pans.

5. Spoon half of the melted butter over each cake and gently spread it with a spatula so it is evenly distributed.

You don't want to mix it into the batter, you want to have a thin layer of melted butter over the top. (The layer will not be a smooth one.)

6. Sprinkle half of the cinnamon and sugar mixture over each cake and then sprinkle half of the almonds over each cake.

7. Bake the cakes for 20 minutes or until lightly browned around the edges. Cool the cakes in the pans on wire racks. Cut into 1½-inch-by-3-inch rectangles and arrange on serving plates. Cover the plates with plastic wrap and store at room temperature until the picnic. The cakes could be made in advance and frozen.

CHAMPAGNE MIMOSAS
▼▼▼▼▼▼▼▼▼▼▼▼▼

Serves 8   Preparation Time: 5 minutes

2 bottles champagne, chilled
2 cups chilled orange juice

1. For each glass of champagne, add ¼ cup orange juice. Serve.

FRUIT PUNCH
▼▼▼▼▼▼▼▼▼▼▼▼▼

Serves 18-20   Preparation Time: 15 minutes

one 48-ounce bottle cranberry juice cocktail, chilled
one 1 liter bottle sparkling water, chilled
4 cups chilled pineapple juice
4 cups cold Red Zinger tea (use 6 tea bags)
a ring of ice
1 orange, thinly sliced

1. Just before serving, pour all the ingredients into a punch bowl over the ice. Float the orange slices on top.

CHAMPAGNE TEA PICNIC

Imagine setting out an elegant high tea in the fresh air. Tea *al fresco* may offer you a new experience. Find a lovely spot under a shady tree and take in the tradition of English country homes.

MENU
CUCUMBER SANDWICHES AND TOMATO SANDWICHES*

RHUBARB CONSERVE* WITH MINIATURE MUFFINS*

TANTE LULU'S APPLE CAKE*

ALMOND RINGS*

FRESH STRAWBERRIES AND CREAM

LEMON WATER OR TEA OR CHAMPAGNE

WINE SUGGESTIONS:

An ultrafine Champagne such as Dom Pérignon or Perrier-Jouët Fleur de Champagne or

Taittinger Comtes de Champagne

EXTRA ITEMS TO BRING:

A TABLE AND CHAIRS, IF YOU WISH TO EMULATE THE BRITISH

LINEN TABLECLOTH AND NAPKINS

FLOWERS

CHINA, SILVERWARE, AND GLASSWARE

CROQUET SET

CUCUMBER SANDWICHES AND TOMATO SANDWICHES
▼▼▼▼▼▼▼▼▼▼▼▼▼

Makes 8 sandwiches   Preparation Time: 30 minutes

1 loaf uncut bread
¼ cup softened butter
8 ounces softened cream cheese
1 cucumber, peeled and thinly sliced
freshly ground black pepper
3 medium tomatoes, cored, peeled, and cut into quarters
salt and pepper to taste

1. Thinly slice the loaf into sixteen slices. Spread each piece of bread out to the edge with a thin layer of butter. Trim the crusts off the slices of bread, so that the edges are even.

2. Spread eight of the bread slices with a thin layer of cream cheese.

3. On four of these cream cheese slices, arrange the cucumbers, and sprinkle with the pepper. Top all four with a buttered slice of bread and with a sharp knife, cut each sandwich into quarters.

4. Remove everything from the tomato quarters except the outer layer of the tomato. On each of the remaining four cream cheese slices of bread, arrange three of these tomato pieces, which will have no seeds or juice and be relatively flat. Sprinkle the tomatoes with the salt and pepper and cover with a buttered slice. Again cut each sandwich into quarters.

5. Place all the sandwiches on a pretty platter, cover with plastic wrap, and store in the refrigerator until tea time. At serving time, garnish the platter with a flower.

RHUBARB CONSERVE
▼▼▼▼▼▼▼▼▼▼▼▼▼

This old family favorite is also delicious with hot or cold meats.

Makes 5 cups   Preparation Time: 30 minutes   Standing Time: Overnight

1 quart rhubarb, cut into 1-inch pieces
2¼ cups sugar
1 orange, finely chopped
1 lemon, finely chopped
1 cup raisins
½ cup coarsely chopped walnuts

1. Place all of the ingredients in a large pot and stir to mix. Let the mixture stand overnight. In the morning, bring the mixture to a boil and cook over medium heat for 15 to 20 minutes or until thick.

2. Place two cups of the conserve in a pretty jar and refrigerate until packing time. Store the remaining conserve in covered containers in the freezer.

MINIATURE MUFFINS
▼▼▼▼▼▼▼▼▼▼▼▼▼▼

These eggless muffins are quite delicious.

Makes 30 small muffins   *Preparation Time: 30 minutes*

1⅔ cups all-purpose flour
⅓ cup wheat germ
¾ cup sugar
½ teaspoon baking soda
¼ teaspoon baking powder
¼ teaspoon salt
1¼ cups buttermilk
3 tablespoons melted butter

1. Preheat the oven to 400° F.

2. Mix all the dry ingredients together in a large bowl.

3. Combine the buttermilk and butter, add to the flour mixture and stir until the mixture is just moistened.

4. Pour the batter into greased small-size muffin pans and bake for 12 to 15 minutes, or until the muffins are slightly browned on the edges.

5. Cool for a few minutes on a wire rack before removing the muffins from the pan.

TANTE LULU'S APPLE CAKE
▼▼▼▼▼▼▼▼▼▼▼▼▼

Makes 1 cake   *Preparation Time: 30 minutes*   *Chilling Time: 2 hours*   *Baking Time: 1 hour*

CRUST:
1 cup softened butter
3 tablespoons sugar
1 egg yolk, slightly beaten
1½ cups all-purpose flour

FILLING:
6 cups apples, peeled, cored, and thinly sliced
1 tablespoon butter
¾ cup sugar
2 tablespoons lemon juice

1. Place the butter, sugar, egg yolk, and flour in a large bowl and mix together with a wooden spoon until the ingredients are combined.

2. Pat the dough in the bottom and up the sides of a springform pan. Chill the dough for 2 hours.

3. To make the filling, place the apples, butter, sugar, and lemon juice in a large pot. Stir the mixture to blend and let sit for 5 minutes to draw the juice from the apples. Cover the pot and steam the apples over low heat for 5 minutes, or until the apples are slightly soft. Cool the apples to room temperature in the pot.

4. Preheat the oven to 325° F.

5. Pour the steamed apples into the chilled crust and bake for 1 hour or until lightly browned around the edges. Cool the cake on a wire rack for 10 minutes. Remove the outer ring and cool the cake completely. Leave the cake on the pan bottom, place on a lace or paper doily, and put in a covered box for transporting to the picnic.

ALMOND RINGS
▼▼▼▼▼▼▼▼▼▼▼▼▼

Makes 16 rings   *Preparation Time: 35 minutes*   *Chilling Time: 1 hour*   *Baking Time: 10 minutes*

¾ cup softened butter
1 egg yolk
¼ cup sugar
½ teaspoon pure almond extract
2 cups all-purpose flour
¼ teaspoon salt
1 egg white, slightly beaten
½ cup ground almonds

1. In a large bowl, place the butter, egg yolk, sugar, and almond extract and mix well with a wooden spoon. Add the flour and salt. Mix thoroughly until the mixture is well blended.

2. Chill the dough for 1 hour.

3. Preheat the oven to 350° F.

4. Break off pieces of the dough the size of a walnut and roll into long rolls like a thick pencil. Form the dough into rings and dip in the egg white. Sprinkle the grated almonds on top and place on an ungreased baking sheet. Bake for 10 minutes or until lightly browned. Remove from the baking sheets and cool on wire racks. Pack in a tightly covered container.

GARDEN PICNIC

Public gardens may not be the ideal spot for your picnic. Instead, select a secluded private garden, possibly in your own backyard or in a field of wildflowers. Let Monet be your guide in creating an elegant garden picnic.

MENU
COLD CARROT SOUP*

MEDITERRANEAN CHICKEN SALAD*

DILLY BREAD*

FOOD FOR THE GODS*

CHILLED WHITE WINE

WINE SUGGESTIONS:

A fine Soave or Pinot Grigio from Northern Italy or a Corvo White from Sicily

EXTRA ITEMS TO BRING:

MORE FLOWERS

INSECT REPELLENT

COLD CARROT SOUP
▼▼▼▼▼▼▼▼▼▼▼▼▼

Serves 8   Preparation Time: 30 minutes   Chilling Time: 2 hours

3 cups peeled and sliced carrots
½ cup water
1 medium onion, chopped
1 tablespoon vegetable oil
1 tablespoon butter
3 cups chicken stock (homemade, if possible)
1 teaspoon peeled and grated fresh gingerroot, or
1 tablespoon finely minced fresh dill
¾ teaspoon salt
¼ teaspoon white pepper
1 cup plain yogurt
dill sprigs for garnish

1. Cook the carrots in the water in a microwave oven for 5 minutes or until tender.

2. Sauté the onion in the oil and butter in a small skillet over medium heat.

3. Pour half of the carrots and onions into a blender with 1 cup of the chicken stock and puree until smooth. Repeat this procedure and add the gingerroot or dill, salt, and pepper to the second batch.

4. Stir the remaining chicken stock and yogurt into the soup and chill for 2 hours. Serve the soup in small bowls and garnish each with a dill sprig.

MEDITERRANEAN CHICKEN SALAD
▼▼▼▼▼▼▼▼▼▼▼▼▼

Serves 8 Preparation Time: 45 minutes

8 chicken breast halves
cold water to cover
1 medium green pepper, seeded and cut into ½-inch chunks
1 small red bell pepper, seeded and cut into ½-inch chunks
1 medium purple onion, cut into ¼-inch chunks
½ cup black olives
¼ cup artichoke hearts
4 leaves fresh basil, chopped
¼ teaspoon salt
freshly ground black pepper
2 tablespoons balsamic vinegar
2 tablespoons olive oil
2 tablespoons corn oil

1. Place the chicken breasts in a large pot and barely cover with cold water. Bring the water to a boil over high heat. Turn down the heat and simmer the chicken for 20 minutes or until just cooked through. Let the chicken cool slightly in the liquid.

2. When the chicken can be handled, remove the meat from the bones and cut into 1-inch chunks. Place the chicken in a large bowl.

3. Add the peppers, onion, olives, artichoke hearts, basil, salt, and pepper to the chicken and stir well. Sprinkle the vinegar and oils over all and stir again. Place the salad in a large covered container and chill in the refrigerator until it is time to pack it in the cooler.

DILLY BREAD
▼▼▼▼▼▼▼▼▼▼▼▼▼

An easy yeast bread that is always a big favorite.

Makes 1 loaf   Preparation Time: 20 minutes
Rising Time: 1 hour 40 minutes   Baking Time: 40 to 50 minutes

1 tablespoon active dry yeast
¼ cup warm water
1 cup low-fat cottage cheese
2 tablespoons sugar
1 tablespoon minced dried onion
2 tablespoons dill seed
¼ teaspoon baking soda
1 egg, slightly beaten
1 tablespoon softened butter or margarine
2¼ to 2½ cups all-purpose flour

1. Sprinkle the yeast over the warm water in a large bowl and let it dissolve.

2. In a medium-size saucepan, gently heat the cottage cheese over low heat until lukewarm, stirring constantly. Add the sugar, onion, dill seed, baking soda, egg, and butter to the cottage cheese. Stir well.

3. Add the cheese mixture to the yeast and mix well. Gradually add the flour, ½ cup at a time, beating with a wooden spoon after each addition. Knead the dough about 10 times in the bowl to work the last of the flour into the dough.

4. Shape the dough into a ball and cover the bowl with a damp cloth. Let the dough rise for about 1 hour, or until it is double in size. Punch down the dough and again shape it into a ball. Place it in a greased 1½-quart round casserole and let it rise for 30 to 40 minutes more.

5. Preheat the oven to 350° F.

6. Bake for 40 to 50 minutes or until lightly browned on top and hollow sounding when tapped. Let the bread rest in the casserole for about 5 minutes before removing it. Cool completely on a wire rack before slicing. Wrap the sliced loaf in a plastic bag and pack in your picnic basket when ready.

FOOD FOR THE GODS
▼▼▼▼▼▼▼▼▼▼▼▼▼

Serves 8 generously   *Preparation Time: 25 minutes*   *Baking Time: 15 to 20 minutes*

3 egg yolks, beaten
7 graham crackers, rolled into crumbs
½ cup sugar
1 teaspoon baking powder
1 cup chopped pecans
½ cup chopped pitted dates
3 egg whites, beaten until stiff peaks form
1 cup heavy cream, whipped (optional)

1. Preheat the oven to 350° F.

2. Place the egg yolks in a large bowl. Add the graham cracker crumbs, sugar, baking powder, pecans, and dates and mix well. Gently fold the egg whites into the crumb mixture until combined.

3. Pour the batter into two greased 9-inch-by-13-inch baking pans. Bake for 15 to 20 minutes or until lightly browned. Cool on wire racks for 10 minutes before cutting.

4. Put the pieces on a plate and cover with plastic wrap for traveling to the picnic.

ROMANTIC PICNICS

Picnics are made for lovers. The familiar phrase, "a jug of wine , a loaf of bread and Thou" which evokes the essence of a romantic picnic dates back to the Persian Omar Khayyám in the eleventh century. Modern day picnickers are practicing an ancient human activity.

BREAKFAST IN A MEADOW PICNIC

Imagine it: A lovely lazy sunny morning with a pile of Sunday papers and delicious food to nibble on as the morning passes. Pack a beautiful basket of goodies that two of you can carry easily as you trudge to your meadow.

MENU

FRESH STRAWBERRIES DIPPED IN CONFECTIONERS' SUGAR

COUNTRY PÂTÉ* AND ASSORTED CRACKERS

IMPORTED CHEESES

SUNNY MORNING MUFFINS* WITH SWEET BUTTER

SWISS CHOCOLATE ALMOND COFFEE

CHAMPAGNE

WINE SUGGESTIONS:

A lighter French champagne such as Perrier Jouët or a Crémant D'Alsace or a reasonably priced Spanish Sparkling Wine

EXTRA ITEMS TO BRING:

BLANKETS

BEACH CHAIRS

COUNTRY PÂTÉ
▼▼▼▼▼▼▼▼▼▼▼▼▼

This tasty pâté does not take long to make, but it requires some planning ahead.

Serves 8   *Marinating Time: 2 hours*   *Preparation Time: 20 minutes*
Baking Time: 1½ to 2 hours   *Storage Time: 2 days*

1¼ pounds chicken livers
6 tablespoons port wine
dash dried thyme
2 bay leaves, crumbled
4 slices imported ham
¾ pound bulk sausage
3 slices bread, soaked in ½ cup milk
½ cup dry white wine
1 garlic clove, minced
freshly ground black pepper
6 strips bacon
2 bay leaves, whole

1. Preheat the oven to 375° F.

2. Rinse the chicken livers in cold water and pat dry. Place them in a bowl with the port, thyme, and crumbled bay leaves and marinate in the refrigerator for 2 hours.

3. Remove the bay leaves from the marinade and put ¾ of the chicken livers and the marinade in a food processor. Reserve the remaining livers. Add the ham, sausage, and bread. Process until you have a coarse mixture. Stir in the wine, garlic, and pepper.

4. Line a square 8-inch-by-8-inch glass baking pan or a 9-inch-by-5-inch glass pâté pan with 3 slices of the bacon. Spread half of the liver sausage mixture in the pan. Add the reserved whole livers and cover with the remaining liver sausage mixture. Top the pâté with the remaining bacon and the whole bay leaves.

5. Cover the pan and place in a larger pan of boiling water and bake for 1½ to 2 hours. Remove from the oven, pour off the juices, and place a weight on the pâté as it cools in the refrigerator. Wrap the cold pâté in plastic wrap and store in the refrigerator for 2 days before serving.

SUNNY MORNING MUFFINS
▼▼▼▼▼▼▼▼▼▼▼▼▼

Makes 15 muffins   Preparation Time: 20 minutes   Baking Time: 25 to 30 minutes

1½ cups unbleached all-purpose flour
½ cup whole-wheat flour
¾ cup sugar
2 teaspoons ground cinnamon
2 teaspoons baking soda
½ teaspoon salt
3 eggs, slightly beaten
¾ cup vegetable oil
2 cups grated carrots, or zucchini, or a combination
½ cup chopped pecans
½ cup golden raisins
½ cup coconut (optional)
½ cup undrained crushed pineapple

1. Preheat the oven to 350° F.

2. Sift the two flours with the sugar, cinnamon, baking soda, and salt into a large bowl. In a small bowl, mix the eggs and oil together and add to the flour mixture. Stir the batter just until the dry ingredients are moistened.

3. Fold the carrots, pecans, raisins, coconut, and pineapple into the batter and stir until blended.

4. Pour the batter into greased muffin pans and bake for 25 to 30 minutes, or until a tester inserted in the center of a muffin comes out clean. Cool the muffins in the pans on a wire rack for 10 minutes. Remove the muffins from the pan and wrap four of them in a napkin. Put them in the picnic basket and hope that they will be still warm when you get to your meadow.

SUNLIGHT THROUGH THE TREES PICNIC

Deep woods with tall trees filter the sunlight onto soft grass in a sheltered glade. A meandering stream gently gurgling over rocks provides the background music. You are at the perfect secluded spot for a romantic picnic.

MENU

TORTELLINI CHICKEN SALAD*

CITRUS SALAD*

BLUEBERRY MUFFINS*

LEMON SAND TORTE WITH FRUIT*

CHILLED WHITE WINE

WINE SUGGESTIONS:

A fine Muscadet or a dry Chenin Blanc from Washington State or a Portuguese Vinta Verde

EXTRA ITEMS TO BRING:

OLD QUILT

GROUND CLOTH

INSECT REPELLENT

WINE GLASSES

CLOTH NAPKINS

TORTELLINI CHICKEN SALAD
▼▼▼▼▼▼▼▼▼▼▼▼▼

This is such a delicious salad that the recipe is for eight servings even though we assume only two will go on this romantic picnic. You will have no trouble using up the remaining salad.

Serves 8   Preparation Time: 45 minutes

6 chicken breast halves
cold water to cover
2 tablespoons olive oil
2 garlic cloves, minced
9 ounces fresh tortellini pasta
1 medium green pepper, seeded and chopped
3 stalks celery, sliced
1 medium purple onion, chopped
¼ pound smoked Gruyère cheese, cut into ½-inch cubes
½ teaspoon salt
freshly ground black pepper

VINAIGRETTE:
¾ cup cider vinegar
¼ cup honey
2 tablespoons Dijon mustard
1 teaspoon dry mustard
¾ cup corn oil

1. Place the chicken breasts in a large pot and barely cover with the cold water. Bring the water to a boil over high heat. Turn down the heat and simmer the chicken for 15 minutes or until barely cooked through. Let the chicken cool slightly in the liquid.

2. When the chicken can be handled, remove the meat from the bones and cut into ½-inch-by-3-inch strips.

3. Heat the olive oil in a large skillet, add the garlic, and sauté until golden brown. Remove the garlic and reserve. Add the chicken to the skillet and sauté for 1 minute, stirring constantly.

4. Cook the tortellini in a large pot of boiling water according to the directions on the package. Drain and rinse quickly in cold water.

5. Place the chicken, reserved garlic, tortellini, pepper, celery, cheese, onion, salt, and pepper in a large bowl and toss together.

6. To make the vinaigrette, place the vinegar, honey, and both mustards in a blender or food processor and process until blended. Slowly drizzle in the oil while the motor is running and blend until creamy. Pour over the salad and stir well.

7. Pack two generous cups of the salad into a covered container and chill in the refrigerator until it is time to pack the cooler. Cover the remaining salad and serve to family or friends.

CITRUS SALAD
▼▼▼▼▼▼▼▼▼▼▼▼▼

A quick and easy salad that is easy to multiply.

Serves 2   Preparation Time: 15 minutes

4 leaves red leaf lettuce, washed, dried, and crisped
½ small purple onion, thinly sliced
1 orange, peeled and sectioned
1 grapefruit half, peeled and sectioned

MUSTARD VINAIGRETTE:
2 tablespoons Dijon mustard
1 tablespoon white wine tarragon vinegar
1 garlic clove, minced
1 teaspoon sugar
¼ teaspoon salt
freshly ground black pepper
⅓ cup vegetable oil

1. Place the lettuce in a seal-lock plastic bag and chill in the refrigerator.

2. Combine the onion and orange and grapefruit sections in a small bowl. Pack in a tightly covered container and chill in the refrigerator.

3. To make the vinaigrette, whisk together the mustard, vinegar, garlic, sugar, salt, and pepper in a small bowl. Slowly whisk in the oil until the mixture is creamy. Pour the vinaigrette in a small jar with a tight-fitting lid and bring to the picnic.

4. To serve the salad, place some lettuce leaves on each plate, then a serving of the salad, and top with the vinaigrette.

BLUEBERRY MUFFINS
▼▼▼▼▼▼▼▼▼▼▼▼▼▼

Makes 12 muffins   *Preparation Time: 15 minutes*   *Baking Time: 18 minutes*

1⅔ cups all-purpose flour
⅓ cup wheat germ
¾ cup sugar
½ teaspoon salt
1 teaspoon baking soda
1½ cups blueberries (preferably small wild ones)
1 cup buttermilk
2 tablespoons melted butter
sweet butter to spread on the muffins

1. Preheat the oven to 400°F.

2. In a large bowl, combine the flour, wheat germ, sugar, salt, and baking soda. Add the blueberries and stir to coat the berries. Add the buttermilk and butter and stir until just mixed.

3. Spoon the batter into greased muffin pans and bake for 18 minutes or until golden brown. Cool in the pans for 2 minutes. Remove from the pans and cool completely on a wire rack.

4. Pack four of the muffins in a plastic bag for the picnic. Pack a small container of sweet butter to serve with them.

LEMON SAND TORTE WITH FRUIT
▼▼▼▼▼▼▼▼▼▼▼▼▼

This rich, old-fashioned German cake recipe comes from a friend of my grandmother's and was enjoyed at many a "kaffee klatch."

Makes 1 cake   Preparation Time: 20 minutes   Baking Time: 1 hour

2 cups softened butter
1 ¼ cups sugar
2 cups all-purpose flour
1 teaspoon baking powder
5 eggs
2 tablespoons grated lemon rind
1 quart fresh strawberries

1. Preheat the oven to 350° F.

2. In the large bowl of an electric mixer, cream the butter and sugar until light and fluffy.

3. In a small bowl, combine the flour and baking powder.

4. With the mixer at low speed, add the eggs to the butter mixture, one at a time, beating after each egg. Add some of the flour mixture after each egg until all the eggs and all the flour are in the batter. Add the lemon rind and continue beating for 1 minute.

5. Pour the batter into a greased and floured tube pan and bake for 1 hour, or until golden brown on top and a tester inserted in the center comes out clean.

6. Cool the cake for 10 minutes on a wire rack. Remove from the pan and continue cooling on a wire rack. When cool, slice the cake and arrange some of the slices on a picnic plate. Cover with plastic wrap, and then pack in the picnic basket when you are ready to go. Cover the remaining cake and enjoy at another time. You may also double wrap the remaining cake and store in the freezer.

7. Rinse the strawberries and leave the hulls on. Place them in a seal-lock plastic bag and pack in the cooler. Serve them alongside the cake.

MOONLIGHT ON A MOUNTAINTOP PICNIC

On a mountaintop, bright moonlight casts a glow of romance and wonder. Food may not be necessary, but for hungry lovers here is a romantic menu. Pack the food in attractive little containers, don't bring too much, and put it all in an old-fashioned romantic picnic basket. Choose a mountain that is easy to reach on foot.

MENU

SHRIMP DIP* WITH CRACKERS

ROAST BEEF SALAD*

CRUSTY FRENCH BREAD WITH PESTO BUTTER*

FRESH TOMATO ASPIC WITH LEMON DILL SAUCE*

CHOCOLATE-DIPPED STRAWBERRIES*

RED WINE

WINE SUGGESTIONS:

A California Pinot Noir or a slightly chilled Chinon or Bourgueil from France

EXTRA ITEMS TO BRING:

A FLASHLIGHT, IN CASE THE MOONLIGHT FAILS

BLANKET OR GROUND COVER

FLOWERS

CLOTH NAPKINS

WINE GLASSES

SHRIMP DIP
▼▼▼▼▼▼▼▼▼▼▼▼▼

This delicious dip is quickly concocted and can easily be doubled.

Makes 1 cup   Preparation Time: 15 minutes

¼ pound shrimp, cooked, peeled, deveined, and chopped
½ cup large curd cottage cheese
2 tablespoons chili sauce
½ teaspoon grated onions
½ teaspoon lemon juice
¼ teaspoon Worcestershire sauce
assorted crackers

1. Place all the ingredients in a small bowl and mix well.

2. Place the dip in a small crock and chill. Cover with plastic wrap and pack in an insulated bag. Serve with the crackers.

ROAST BEEF SALAD
▼▼▼▼▼▼▼▼▼▼▼▼▼

Serves 4   Preparation Time: 15 minutes

4 cups cooked, cold London broil or flank steak, thinly sliced and julienned
¼ cup balsamic vinegar
2 teaspoons horseradish
1 small purple onion, thinly sliced
6 sun-dried tomatoes, julienned
1 tablespoon olive oil
2 tablespoons sesame oil
¼ teaspoon salt
freshly ground black pepper

1. Mix all the ingredients together in a large bowl.

2. Place in a covered container and chill until time to pack it in your insulated bag.

FRENCH BREAD WITH PESTO BUTTER
▼▼▼▼▼▼▼▼▼▼▼▼▼▼

Serves 2 or more   *Preparation Time: 20 minutes*

¼ cup pesto
½ cup softened sweet butter
1 loaf fresh crusty French bread

1. Preheat the oven to 350° F.

2. Mix the pesto and butter together in a small bowl.

3. Slice the bread crosswise and spread the butter on one cut side.

4. Wrap the bread in aluminum foil and place in the oven for 15 minutes, just before leaving for the picnic.

5. Wrap the warm loaf in a tablecloth and pack it in your picnic basket. Break off hunks of bread to eat with the *Roast Beef Salad.*

FRESH TOMATO ASPIC WITH LEMON DILL SAUCE
▼▼▼▼▼▼▼▼▼▼▼▼▼

Serves 8   Preparation Time: 15 minutes   Chilling Time: 2 hours

2 tablespoons unflavored gelatin
2 tablespoons cold water
½ cup boiling water
2 cups tomato juice
1 tablespoon lemon juice
½ teaspoon finely cut fresh dill
1 cup seeded and chopped tomatoes

LEMON DILL SAUCE:
1 tablespoon finely cut fresh dill
1 tablespoon lemon juice
3 tablespoons mayonnaise
¼ cup plain yogurt

1. In a small bowl, dissolve the gelatin in the cold water. Add the boiling water and stir until the gelatin is totally dissolved.

2. Add the remaining ingredients and mix well. Pour the aspic into two ½-cup molds and one 1-quart mold and chill for 2 hours. Cover the two small molds with aluminum foil and pack in your insulated bag when it is time to leave.

3. To make the sauce, combine all the ingredients in a small bowl and gently whisk until they are just combined. Pour about ¼ cup of the sauce in a small jar with a tight-fitting lid and chill until time to put it in your insulated bag. Chill the remaining sauce in another container to serve with the larger mold later.

CHOCOLATE-DIPPED STRAWBERRIES
▼▼▼▼▼▼▼▼▼▼▼▼▼

Strawberries keep best if they are unwashed and have their stems on. For these luscious dipped strawberries, keep the green tops on.

Makes 1 cup   Preparation Time: 30 minutes

1 cup semisweet chocolate chips, melted
(Do not let the chocolate get hot, around 110° F. is perfect.
A microwave oven is useful for this step.)
2 tablespoons melted butter
3 tablespoons Grand Marnier liqueur
¼ cup confectioners' sugar
1 tablespoon water
selected large fresh strawberries, washed and patted dry

1. Combine the chocolate, butter, and Grand Marnier in a small bowl and whisk together.

2. Add the confectioners' sugar and water and continue whisking until smooth.

3. Dip the strawberries about three-quarters of the way into the chocolate. Let them drain on wax paper and sit until the chocolate has set. Pack them carefully in a small-lidded tin, lined with wax paper. They don't keep for long — make them the day you plan to have your picnic.

INDEX

▼▼

A
Almond rings, 150
Almond tart, 24
Apple cake: Tante Lulu's, 149
Apple pie: sour cream, 109
Artichoke salad, 71
Asparagus: chilled asparagus, 120
Avocado: guacamole, 50

B
Baked brie with fresh fruit, 105
Barbecued butterfly lamb, 88
Barbecued chicken: chicken, 62-63
Beans: eight bean salad, 64-65;
    green beans and tomatoes, 77;
    hummus, 69; spicy beans with
    sausage, 76-77; ten bean soup,
    26
Berry: cold berry soup, 42
Blueberry muffins, 164
Blueberry peach tart, 45-46
Bodil's almond tart, 24
Borscht, 20
Boursin, 21
Bread: Caretaker Farm bread, 27-
    28; dilly bread, 154; French
    bread with pesto butter, 169;
    gingerbread, 33; honey whole-
    wheat bread, 51-52; Mexican
    cornbread, 78; primavera, 43-44;
    tomato basil bread, 102;
    zesty rye, 22-23

Brie: baked brie with fresh fruit, 105
Broccoli salad with Caesar
    dressing, 108
Broccoli soup, 93
Brownies, 79; raspberry
    brownies, 102
Bundt cake, 53
Butter: lemon butter, 131

C
Caesar dressing: broccoli salad
    with, 108
Cake: blueberry-peach tart, 45-46;
    Bodil's almond tart, 24; brown
    ies,79; bundt cake, 53; carrot
    cake with orange cream
    cheeseicing, 85; chocolate lush,
    74; chocolate zucchini cake, 73;
    gingerbread, 33; Gramma Bea's
    strawberry shortcake, 66-67;
    Omi's cocoa cake, 127-28;
    raspberry brownies, 103; sour
    cream chocolate cake, 114-15;
    Tante Lulu's apple cake, 149;
    Tante's coffee cake, 143
Calzones: picnic, 55-56
Caretaker Farm bread, 27
Carrot cake with orange cream
    cheese icing, 85
Carrots: carrots with minted
    mustard vinaigrette, 90; cold
    carrot soup, 152; with minted
    mustard vinaigrette, 90; shred

ded carrots with walnut vinai-
    grette, 111
Casserole: cheese casserole, 119
Champagne framboise, 96
Champagne mimosas, 144
Cheese: baked brie with fresh fruit,
    105; boursin, 21
Cheese casserole, 119
Chicken: barbecued chicken, 62-63;
    chicken fillets on deli rolls, 32
Chinese chicken salad with fried
    won tons, 136-37; lemony, 37;
    Mediterranean chicken salad,
    153; sesame chicken wings, 112;
    tortellini chicken salad, 161-62
Chicken fillets on deli rolls, 32
Chili: soup and yams, 99
Chilled asparagus, 120
Chinese chicken salad with fried
    won tons, 136-37
Chocolate cake: sour cream, 114-15
Chocolate chip: chocolate chip
    oatmeal cookies, 28; prize
    winning chocolate chip cookies,
    58
Chocolate lush, 74
Chocolate zucchini cake, 73
Chocolate-dipped strawberries, 171
Chowder: corn, 31
Citrus salad, 163
Cocoa cake: Omi's, 127-28
Coffee cake, 143
Cold berry soup, 42

Cold carrot soup, 152
Cold rice salad, 89
Cold zucchini soup, 135
Cold zucchini and tomatoes, 57
Cookies: Kate and Meg's chocolate
    chip oatmeal cookies, 28; pecan
    bars, 138; prize winning
    chocolate chip cookies, 58;
    strawberry, 91; tannies, 39
Corn chowder, 31
Corn pudding, 130
Cornbread: Mexican, 78
Country pâté, 158
Cranberry juice, 40
Creamy horseradish cucumbers, 84
Cucumber: iced soup, 36
Cucumber and tomato sandwiches,
    146
Cucumbers: creamy horseradish
    cucumbers, 84
Currant oat scones, 118

D

Dessert: brownies, 79; chocolate
    lush, 74; currant oat scones,
    118; phyllo turnovers, 122; rasp-
    berry brownies, 102; sour
    cream apple pie, 109; sour
    cream chocolate cake, 114
Dill sauce: grilled salmon fillets
    with, 70; lemon, 170
Dilly bread, 154
Dip: shrimp dip, 167

E

Eight bean salad, 64

F

Flank steak: marinated, 82
Food for the gods, 155
French bread with pesto butter, 169
Fresh fruit bowl kaleidoscope, 142
Fresh lemonade, 96
Fresh pea soup, 49
Fresh peach ice cream, 126
Fresh tomato aspic with lemon dill
    sauce, 170
Fruit: Fruit fresh fruit bowl kaleido-
    scope, 142
Fruit conserves: Roast pork loin
    with mustard and, 106
Fruit punch, 144
Fruit salad: Vonnie's frosty, 72

G

Garbanzo beans: hummus, 69
Garden fresh tomatoes with basil
    and balsamic vinegar, 124
Gazpacho, 87
Gingerbread, 33
Gramma Bea's strawberry short-
    cake, 66
Green beans and tomatoes, 77
Grilled salmon fillets with mustard
    dill sauce, 70
Grilled tuna with lime, 123
Guacamole, 50

H

Herbal iced tea, 34

Honey whole-wheat bread, 51
Horseradish: creamy horseradish
    cucumbers, 84
Hot spiced tea, 29
Hot spiced wine, 80
Huge tossed salad, 95
Hummus, 69

I

Ice cream: fresh peach ice cream,
    126
Iced borscht, 20
Iced cucumber soup, 36
Iced herbal tea, 34

K

Kate and Meg's chocolate chip
    oatmeal cookies, 28

L

Lamb: barbecued butterfly lamb, 88
Lemon butter, 131
Lemon sand torte with fruit, 165
Lemonade: fresh, 96
Lemony chicken, 37
Lettuce: red lettuce salad, 131
Lobster rolls, 94

M

Marinated flank steak, 82
Marinated pasta salad, 125
Mediterranean chicken salad, 153
Mediterranean torte, 107
Mexican cornbread, 78
Mimosas: champagne mimosas, 144
Miniature muffins, 148

Mousse: orange mousse, 132
Muffins: blueberry muffins, 164; miniature, 148; sunny morning muffins, 159
Mustard vinaigrette: carrots with minted, 90

O

Oat: currant oat scones, 118
Oatmeal cookies: chocolate chip, 28
Omi's cocoa cake, 127
Orange cream cheese icing: carrot cake with, 85
Orange mousse, 132
Oriental vegetable salad, 100

P

Pasta: marinated pasta salad, 125; pasta primavera, 101
Pasta primavera, 101
Pâté: country pate, 158
Pea: fresh pea soup, 49
Peach: blueberry peach tart, 45-46; fresh peach ice cream, 126
Pecan bars, 138
Pesto butter: with French bread, 169
Phyllo turnovers, 122
Picnic calzones, 55-56
Picnics: after the wedding brunch, 140; on an island, 86; in autumn, 19, 129; backpacking, 18; backyard family celebration picnics, 60; at beach, 116, 121, 129; berry-picking, 41; breakfast in a meadow, 157; California wine country, 98; champagne tea picnic, 145; elegant, 133; environmental concerns, 12; fall foliage in New England, 104; garden picnics, 151; history of, 9; moonlight on a mountaintop, 166; mountainside picnic, 81; music festival, 134; packing for, 11-13; poolside, 68; potluck picnics, 59; romantic, 156; ski picnics, 25, 75; sports booster, 92; in spring, 30, 48, 117; store-bought, 97; in summer, 35, 110, 121; in winter, 25, 54, 75; workday, 47
Pie: sour cream apple pie, 109; zucchini and sausage pie, 141
Pinenuts: tortellini salad with, 113
Pork: roast pork loin with mustard and conserves, 106
Potato salad: red potato salad with fresh peas, 38
Primavera: pasta, 101
Primavera bread, 43-44
Prize winning chocolate chip cookies, 58
Pudding: corn pudding, 130
Punch: fruit punch, 144

R

Raspberry brownies, 102
Raspberries: champagne framboise, 96
Raspberry: brownies, 103
Red lettuce salad, 131
Red potato salad with fresh peas, 38
Rhubarb conserve, 147
Rice: cold rice salad, 89
Roast beef salad, 168
Roast pork loin with mustard and conserves, 106
Rolls: lobster rolls, 94
Rye bread, 22-23

S

Salad: artichoke, 71; broccoli salad with Caesar dressing, 108; Chinese chicken salad with fried won tons, 136; citrus salad, 163; cold rice salad, 89; eight bean salad, 64; huge tossed salad, 95; marinated pasta salad, 125; Mediterranean chicken salad, 153; Oriental vegetable salad, 100; red lettuce salad, 131; red potato with fresh peas, 38; roast beef salad, 168; tabouli, 83; taco salad, 61; tortellini chicken salad, 161-62; tortellini salad with pinenuts, 113; Vonnie's frosty fruit salad, 72
Salmon: grilled salmon fillets with mustard dill sauce, 78
Sandwiches: cucumber sandwiches and tomato sandwiches, 146; history of, 9
Sangria, 120
Sauce: dill and grilled salmon fillets, 70; lemon dill, 170
Sausage: pie and zucchini, 141; spicy beans with, 76-77

Scones: currant oat scones, 118
Sesame chicken wings, 112
Shredded carrots with walnut
    vinaigrette, 111
Shrimp dip, 167
Soup: broccoli soup, 93; cold berry,
    42; cold carrot soup, 152; cold
    zucchini soup, 135; corn
    chowder, 31; fresh pea soup, 49;
    gazpacho, 87; iced cucumber
    soup, 36; ten bean, 26; yam and
    chili soup, 99
Sour cream apple pie, 109
Sour cream chocolate cake, 114-15
Sparkling cranberry juice, 40
Spicy beans with sausage, 76-77
Steak: marinated flank steak, 82
Strawberries: chocolate-dipped
    strawberries, 171
Strawberry cookies, 91
Strawberry shortcake, 66-67
Sun tea, 139
Sunny morning muffins, 159

T

Tabouli, 83
Taco salad, 61
Tannies, 39
Tante Lulu's apple cake, 149
Tante's coffee cake, 143
Tart: blueberry-peach tart, 45-46;
    Bodil's almond, 24
Tea: herbal iced tea, 34; hot spiced,
    29; sun tea, 139
Ten bean soup, 26
Tomato basil bread, 102

Tomatoes: aspic with lemon dill
    sauce, 170; cold zucchini and
    tomatoes, 57; cucumber
    sandwiches and tomato sand-
    wiches, 146; garden fresh
    tomatoes with basil and
    balsamic vinegar, 124; green
    beans and tomatoes, 77
Torte: lemon sand torte with fruit,
    165; Mediterranean torte, 107;
    Omi's cocoa cake, 127-28
Tortellini chicken salad, 161-62
Tortellini salad with pinenuts, 113
Tuna: grilled tuna with lime, 123
Turnover: phyllo turnovers, 122

V

Vegetable: oriental vegetable salad,
    100
Vonnie's frosty fruit salad, 72

W

Walnut vinaigrette: shredded
    carrots with, 111
White wine spritzers, 40
Whole wheat: honey whole-wheat
    bread, 51-52
Wine: hot spiced wine, 80; sangria,
    120; white wine spritzers, 40
Won tons, 136-37

Y

Yam and chili soup, 99

Z

Zesty rye bread, 22-23
Zucchini: chocolate zucchini cake, 73;
    cold soup, 135; cold zucchini
    and tomatoes, 57; and sausage
    pie, 141